**EXPLORER**

D1076745

# Dubai

## MINI VISITORS' GUIDE

www.explorerpublishing.com

**Dubai** Mini **Visitors'** Guide
ISBN – 978-9948-442-11-0

Copyright © Explorer Group Ltd 2010
All rights reserved.

All maps © Explorer Group Ltd 2010

Front cover photograph: Burj Khalifa – Pete Maloney

Printed and bound by
Emirates Printing Press, Dubai, UAE

**Explorer Publishing & Distribution**
PO Box 34275, Dubai, United Arab Emirates
Phone (+971 4) 340 8805   Fax (+971 4) 340 8806
info@explorerpublishing.com
www.explorerpublishing.com

Welcome to the *Dubai Mini Visitors' Guide*. This mini marvel has been passionately prepared by the same team that brought you the *Dubai Explorer, Live Work Explore*. Written entirely by residents, and perfect for visitors, you'll find all you need to make the most out of your time in this interesting metropolis – whether it is the top restaurants, the most stylish shops or the best cultural spots.

Dubai is a dynamic city, with an ever-changing skyline, and Explorer brings you the insider knowledge on the sights and sounds of this exciting emirate. With the new Dubai Metro system underway, we have indicated the closest metro stations to each location to help you navigate the city. There is a system of feeder buses which takes passengers to locations that are further afield – for more information check out www.rta.ae.

For more info on the metro and other Dubai facts, as well as up-to-the-minute events and exciting new releases from Explorer Publishing, log onto www.explorerpublishing.com/dubai, where you can also give us your own take on this unique city.

**The Explorer Team**

Welcome...

GET IN TOUCH WITH NATURE.
AL AIN WILDLIFE PARK & RESORT.

The Al Ain Wildlife Park & Resort is a place for people who want to experience and learn about wildlife and conservation in a unique natural desert setting. Sustainable, educational and thoroughly entertaining, the Al Ain Wildlife Park & Resort is one of the world's most ambitious wildlife projects and will provide an extraordinary opportunity for visitors to explore the desert world. Our Conservation and Breeding Centre currently runs programmes to protect the Arabian leopard, Addax, Scimitar-horned oryx, Arabian oryx, Sand cat and African lion.

Al Ain Wildlife Park & Resort – In touch with nature.

For opening times and special attractions please visit www.awpr.ae or call 800 AWPR (2977).

متنزه العين
للحياة البرية
AL AIN WILDLIFE
PARK & RESORT

أقرب إلى الطبيعة
In touch with nature

In collaboration with
SAN DIEGO ZOO
CONSERVATION FIRST

# Contents

# Essentials

# Welcome To Dubai

## Welcome to a city of stark contrasts; of sand dunes and skyscrapers, camels and fast cars, museums and malls. Welcome to Dubai.

Whatever your reason for touching down in this desert metropolis, it's hard not to be captivated by its growth and unshakeable ambition. The world's tallest building is already here, and a slew of new towers and whole communities are not far behind. Yet underneath the shiny surface there is more to Dubai than cranes and five-star cliche: you'll find Emiratis, fresh-faced expats, corporate climbers, and sunburnt tourists all enjoying and exploring the many aspects of a surprisingly multi-layered city.

As you'd expect from a truly international destination, there is a wide scope of activities, cuisines and adventures to be had, many at prices that you wouldn't expect from the 'seven-star' headlines. Try dining in Arabic street cafes (p.222), browsing the souks (p.188) and haggling for souvenirs (p.185) to get a sense of local tradition, or sample Dubai's plethora of malls (p.196), upmarket hotels (p.66) and fine-dining restaurants for a taste of its luxury reputation.

Outside the city are a whole new set of landscapes and a more traditional way of life. Seemingly endless vistas of untouched sand dunes are just waiting to be explored, so pile into that Land Cruiser and take a tour. Further out, the East Coast of the UAE (p.128) is a haven for divers and snorkellers,

Sheikh Zayed Road

and the delights of Oman's rugged Musandam peninsula (p.136) are only an hour or so north.

Over the next few pages, descriptions of the local culture and history should provide context to your trip. Following this is the vital information you'll need to get here and stay in style, plus advice on what to do when you first arrive. The things that you really shouldn't miss start on p.20. The Exploring chapter (p.76) divides the city up, highlighting each area's best bits, such as museums, galleries and heritage sites. In Sports & Spas (p.140) you'll find out what the city has to offer for sports fans, keen golfers, and those who simply prefer to be pampered. Shopping (p.176) is your detailed guide to malls, boutiques and souks, and Going Out (p.216) will help you manoeuvre your way through Dubai's increasingly impressive maze of restaurants, bars and clubs.

## Culture & Heritage

# Rapid change and growing multiculturalism hasn't stopped the UAE embracing a proud heritage.

## Development Of Islam

Dubai's early existence is closely linked to the arrival and development of Islam in the greater Middle Eastern region. Islam developed in modern-day Saudi Arabia at the beginning of the seventh century AD with the revelations of the Quran being received by the Prophet Muhammad. Military conquests of the Middle East and North Africa enabled the Arab Empire to spread the teachings of Islam to the local Bedouin tribes. Following the Arab Empire came the Turks, the Mongols and the Ottomans, each leaving their mark on local culture.

## The Trucial States

After the fall of the Muslim empires, both the British and Portuguese became interested in the area due to its strategic position between India and Europe. It also offered an opportunity to control the activities of pirates based in the region, earning it the title the 'Pirate Coast'. In 1820 the British defeated the pirates and a general treaty was agreed with the local rulers, denouncing piracy. The following years witnessed a series of maritime truces, with Dubai and the other emirates accepting British protection in 1892. In Europe, the area became known as the Trucial Coast (or Trucial States), a name it retained until the departure of the British in 1971.

Fishing nets

# Growing Trade

In the late 1800s Dubai's ruler, Sheikh Maktoum bin Hasher Al Maktoum, granted tax concessions to foreign traders, encouraging many to switch their operations from Iran and Sharjah to Dubai. By 1903, a British shipping line had been persuaded to use Dubai as its main port in the area, giving traders direct links with British India and other key ports. Dubai's importance as a trading hub was further enhanced by Sheikh Rashid bin Saeed Al Maktoum, father of the current ruler, who ordered the creek to be dredged to provide access for larger vessels. The city came to specialise in the import and re-export of goods, mainly gold to India, and trade became the foundation of the emirate's wealthy progression.

# Independence

In 1968, Britain announced its withdrawal from the region and oversaw the proposed creation of a single state consisting of Bahrain, Qatar and the Trucial Coast. The ruling sheikhs, particularly of Abu Dhabi and Dubai, realised that by uniting forces they would have a stronger voice in the wider Middle East region. Negotiations collapsed when Bahrain and Qatar chose to become independent states. However, the Trucial Coast remained committed to forming an alliance, and in 1971 the federation of the United Arab Emirates was born.

# Formation Of The UAE

The new state comprised the emirates of Dubai, Abu Dhabi, Ajman, Fujairah, Sharjah, Umm Al Quwain and, in 1972, Ras Al Khaimah. Each emirate is named after its main town.

Under the agreement, the individual emirates each retained a degree of autonomy, with Abu Dhabi and Dubai providing the most input into the federation. The leaders of the new federation elected the ruler of Abu Dhabi, HH Sheikh Zayed bin Sultan Al Nahyan, to be their president, a position he held until he passed away on 2 November 2004. His eldest son, HH Sheikh Khalifa bin Zayed Al Nahyan, was then elected to take over the presidency. Despite the unification of the seven emirates, boundary disputes have caused a few problems. At the end of Sheikh Zayed's first term in 1976, he threatened to resign if the other rulers didn't settle the demarcation of their borders. The threat proved an effective way of ensuring cooperation, although the degree of independence of the various emirates has never been fully determined.

## The Discovery Of Oil

The formation of the UAE came after the discovery of huge oil reserves in Abu Dhabi in 1958. The emirate has an incredible 10% of the world's known oil reserves. This discovery dramatically transformed the emirate. In 1966, Dubai, which was already a relatively wealthy trading centre, also discovered oil.

Dubai's ruler at the time, the late Sheikh Rashid bin Saeed Al Maktoum, ensured that the emirate's oil revenues were used to develop an economic and social infrastructure, which is the basis of today's modern society. His work was continued through the reign of his son, and successor, Sheikh Maktoum bin Rashid Al Maktoum and by the present ruler, Sheikh Mohammed bin Rashid Al Maktoum.

# Culture

Despite Dubai being a modern metropolis, with a cosmopolitan population and mega projects, the emirate is very rooted in its traditions. Culture in Dubai is based on the Islamic customs that deeply penetrate the Arabian Peninsula and beyond. Courtesy and hospitality are the highly prized virtues and visitors are likely to experience the genuine warmth and friendliness of the local people – if you meet them, of course (less than 15% of the population is Emirati).

The rapid economic development over the last 30 years, that was sparked by the reign of Sheikh Zayed bin Sultan Al Nayhan (the 'father of the UAE'), has changed life in the Emirates beyond recognition. However, the country's rulers are committed to safeguarding its heritage. They are keen to promote cultural and sporting events that are representative of the UAE's traditions, such as falconry, camel racing and traditional dhow sailing. Arabic culture, as seen through poetry, dancing, songs and traditional art, is encouraged, and weddings and celebrations are still colourful occasions of feasting and music.

# Food & Drink

Most of the Arabic food available is predominantly based on Lebanese cuisine. Common dishes are shawarmas (lamb or chicken carved from a spit and served in a pita bread with salad and tahina), falafel (mashed chickpeas and sesame seeds, rolled into balls and deep fried), hummus (a creamy dip made from chickpeas and olive oil), and tabbouleh (finely chopped parsley, mint and crushed wheat).

Heritage Village

There are also opportunities to sample Emirati food while in Dubai. The legacy of the UAE's trading past means that local cuisine uses a blend of ingredients imported from Asia and the Middle East. Dried limes are a common ingredient, reflecting a Persian influence; they impart a distinctively musty, tangy, sour flavour to soups and stews. Spices such as cinnamon, saffron and turmeric along with nuts (almonds or pistachios) and dried fruit add interesting flavours to Emirati

dishes. Look out for Al Harees, a celebratory dish made from meat and wheat, slow-cooked in a clay pot or oven for hours, and Al Majboos, in which meat and rice are cooked in a stock made from local spices and dried limes. Fish is widely used in local cuisine, both freshly caught and preserved. Al Madrooba is a dish which uses local salted fish, prepared in a thick, buttery sauce.

Among the most famed Middle Eastern delicacies are dates and coffee. Dates are one of the few crops that thrive naturally throughout the Arab world and date palms have been cultivated in the area for around 5,000 years. The serving of traditional coffee (kahwa) is an important social ritual in the Middle East. Local coffee is mild with a distinctive taste of cardamom and saffron, and it is served black without sugar. It is considered polite to drink about three cups of the coffee when offered.

Muslims are not allowed to eat pork. In order for a restaurant to have pork on its menu, it should have a separate fridge, preparation equipment and cooking area. Supermarkets are also required to sell pork in a separate area. All meat products for Muslim consumption have to be halal, which refers to the method of slaughter.

Alcohol is also considered haram (taboo) in Islam. It is only served in licensed outlets associated with hotels (restaurants and bars), plus a few leisure venues (such as golf clubs) and clubs. Restaurants outside of hotels, that are not part of a club or association, are not permitted to serve alcohol.

## Shisha

Smoking the traditional shisha (water pipe) is a popular and relaxing pastime enjoyed throughout the Middle East. Shisha pipes can be smoked with a variety of aromatic flavours, such as strawberry, grape or apple. The experience is unlike normal cigarette or cigar smoking since the tobacco and molasses are filtered through water. Contrary to what many people think, shisha tobacco contains nicotine and can be addictive.

Despite ongoing rumours that smoking shisha outside will be banned in the UAE it remains hugely popular. See p.222 for some of the best spots.

# Religion

Islam is the official religion of the UAE and is widely practised, however there are people of various nationalities and religions working and living in the region side by side.

In Islam, the family unit is very important and elders are respected for their experience and wisdom. It's common for many generations to live together in the same house.

Muslims are required to pray (facing Mecca) five times a day. Most people pray at a mosque, although it's not unusual to see people kneeling by the side of the road if they are not near a place of worship. The call to prayer, transmitted through loudspeakers on the minarets of each mosque, ensures that everyone knows it's time to pray.

Friday is the Islamic holy day, and the first day of the weekend in Dubai, when most businesses close to allow people to go to the mosque to pray and to spend time with their families. Many shops and tourist attractions have different hours of operation, opening around 14:00 after Friday prayers.

During the holy month of Ramadan, Muslims abstain from all food, drinks, cigarettes and unclean thoughts (or activities) between dawn and dusk for 30 days. In the evening, the fast is broken with the Iftar feast. All over the city, festive Ramadan tents are filled to the brim with people of all nationalities and religions enjoying shisha, traditional Arabic mezze and sweets. The timing of Ramadan is not fixed in terms of the western calendar, but depends on the lunar Islamic calendar.

During Ramadan the sale of alcohol in most outlets is restricted to after dusk, while shops and parks usually open and close later. In addition, no live music or dancing is allowed. Ramadan ends with a three-day celebration and holiday called Eid Al Fitr, the feast of the breaking of the fast.

While the predominant religion in Dubai is Islam, people are freely permitted to practise other religions. The ruling family has, on numerous occasions, donated plots of land for the building of churches. Christian churches of various denominations have been built in clusters on Oud Metha Road (Map 5 A6) and in Jebel Ali, and there is a Hindu temple in Bur Dubai (Map 5 B2).

# National Dress

In general, the local population wear traditional dress in public. For men this is the dishdash(a) or khandura: a white full length shirt dress, which is worn with a white or red checked headdress, known as a gutra. This is secured with a black cord (agal). Sheikhs and important businessmen may also wear a thin black or brown robe (known as a bisht or mishlah), over their dishdasha at important events. You'll sometimes see men wearing a brimless embroidered hat (kumah), which is more common in neighbouring Oman.

In public, women wear the black abaya – a long, loose robe that covers their normal clothes – plus a headscarf called a sheyla. The abaya is often of sheer, flowing fabric and may be open at the front. Some women also wear a thin black veil hiding their face and/or gloves, and some older women wear a leather mask, known as a burkha, which covers the nose, brow and cheekbones. Underneath the abaya, women traditionally wear a long tunic over loose fitting trousers (sirwall), which are normally heavily embroidered and fitted at the wrists and ankles.

**Cross Culture**

The Sheikh Mohammed Centre for Cultural Understanding (p.84) was established to help bridge the gap between cultures and give visitors and residents a clearer appreciation of the Emirati way of life. It organises tours of Jumeira Mosque (p.109), one of the few in the UAE open to non-Muslims (www.cultures.ae).

# Modern Dubai

**Below the glittering towers, the City of Gold is still under construction and is likely to remain so for some time.**

Until 2009, market experts struggled to keep up with the constant stream of announcements for new billion-dollar developments, each striving to out-do the last. However, the city's cranes ground to a halt when the financial crisis hit, leaving the same experts struggling to keep up with the number of cancelled projects announced on a daily basis.

Although the future of some of the city's most ambitious developments remains uncertain, the Dubai of today is nothing like the Dubai of 50 years ago. One of the city's most surprising aspects is its rather modest beginning, but while Dubai takes great pride in its past, it remains firmly focused on the future.

## People & Economy

There are an estimated 150 nationalities living in Dubai. According to a national census, the population in 1968 was 58,971. By 2008, it had grown to 1.6 million. Following the global economic crisis in 2009, it was forecast that Dubai would experience its first population decline in many years. A new census was conducted in April 2010 and updated official statistics are due to be published, but experts estimate a decline of anywhere between 8% and 17%.

Developing Dubai

Expats make up more than 80% of the population. Nearly 75% of expat residents hail from the Asian subcontinent, many of whom work on the construction of the city's massive skyscrapers that have come to define it.

Dubai's economy has been weaning itself off oil dependence for the last few decades. Whereas 20 years ago oil revenues accounted for around half of Dubai's GDP, in 2007 the oil sector contributed just 3%. Today, trade, manufacturing, transport, construction and real estate, finance and tourism are the main contributors.

# Tourism

The development of high-end hotels and visitor attractions, in conjunction with an aggressive overseas marketing campaign, has made Dubai a popular holiday destination. Dubai is striving to reach its target of attracting 15 million visitors a year in 2010 and 40 million by 2015 and, despite tough economic conditions, the number of tourists coming to Dubai is still on the rise. The city's hotels and hotel apartments accommodated 7.5 million guests in 2008, an increase of 7.7% on the previous year. During the first half of 2009, the number of tourists grew by 5% in comparison to the same period of 2008.

# New Developments

Until recently, Dubai's booming economy meant that for every record-breaking mega development that was completed, three new ones were announced. In the wake of the global economic slow-down, some projects have fallen behind their original construction schedules and others have been put on indefinite hold. Despite the gloomy economic conditions, work on many key developments is still going ahead and in 2009 major projects such as the Burj Khalifa (p.27) and the first phase of the Dubai Metro (p.54) were completed.

Work continues on some of Dubai's most ambitious projects including Palm Jebel Ali – the second of the three Palm Islands, Meydan – an urban community centred on a new horseracing track, the vast Dubai Sports City and the residential district of Al Furjan.

Clockwise from left: Space Science World, Burj Khalifa, Sports City

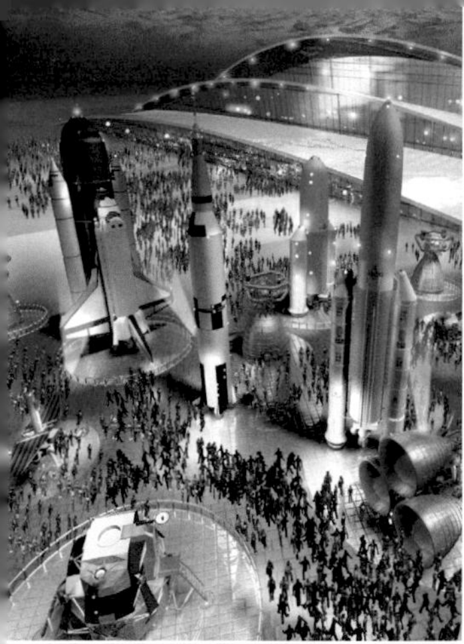

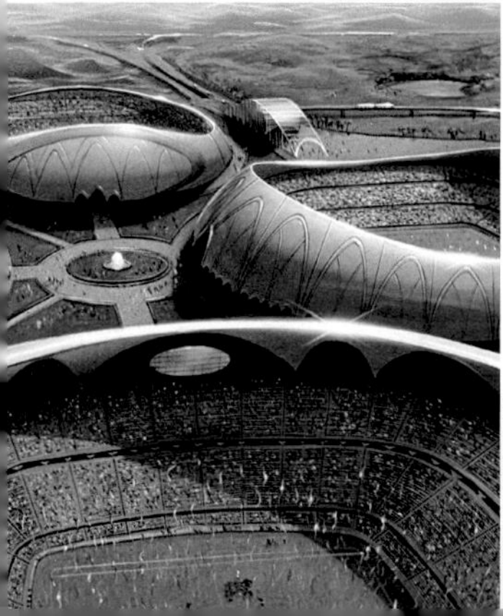

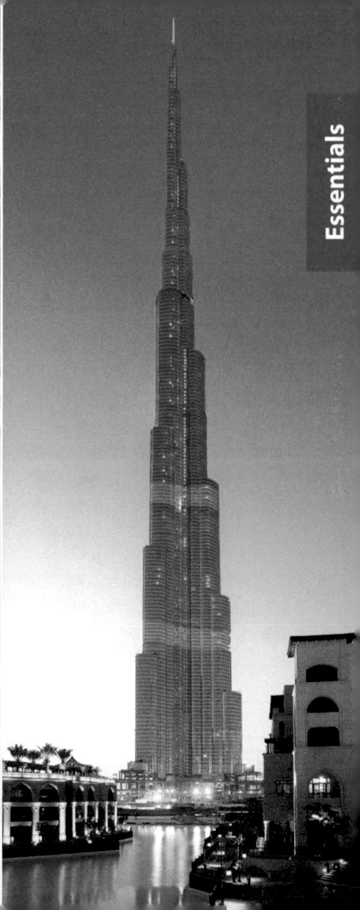

# Dubai Checklist

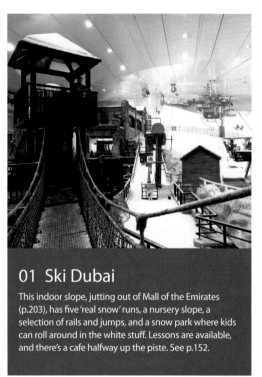

## 01  Ski Dubai

This indoor slope, jutting out of Mall of the Emirates (p.203), has five 'real snow' runs, a nursery slope, a selection of rails and jumps, and a snow park where kids can roll around in the white stuff. Lessons are available, and there's a cafe halfway up the piste. See p.152.

## 02  At The Top, Burj Khalifa

A visit to the world's tallest building is a must. For an interesting perspective of the city, ride the super-fast elevator to the 124th floor for 360° views across Dubai. The viewing deck has special telescopes and there is a well-stocked boutique at the entrance.

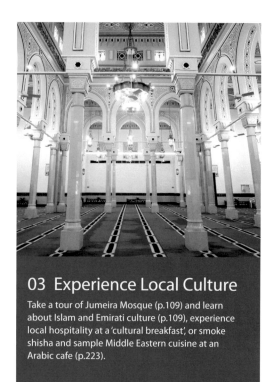

# 03 Experience Local Culture

Take a tour of Jumeira Mosque (p.109) and learn about Islam and Emirati culture (p.109), experience local hospitality at a 'cultural breakfast', or smoke shisha and sample Middle Eastern cuisine at an Arabic cafe (p.223).

## 04 Tackle The Dunes

A trip to the desert is a must during your stay in Dubai. Surfing over the dunes in a car at impossible angles is great fun – as is a camel ride, eating your fill at a barbecue and learning how to belly dance. Tour operators are plentiful and professional. See p.139.

## 05  Sample The Souks

Still an essential part of life for many people, Dubai's
souks are a welcome slice of tradition. Check out the
Spice Souk (p.194), the colourful textile souk in Bur
Dubai (p.195), the Fish Market in Deira and the world-
renowned Gold Souk (p.190).

## 06 Burgeoning Buildings

Splash out on afternoon tea at the Skyview Bar (p.302) at the iconic, sail-shaped Burj Al Arab (p.67). The other burj, the Burj Khalifa, is the world's tallest building and a monument to Dubai's sky high ambition. Survey this remarkable city from the 124th floor.

## 07  Take A Bus Tour

View the city from the upper floor of a double-decker bus, learning some fascinating facts about Dubai along the way. The Big Bus Company (p.139) allows you to hop on and off at various attractions, while the amphibious Wonder Bus takes to water (p.139).

# 08  Hit The Malls

Dubai does shopping bigger and better than most. So whether it's to beat the heat or browse the boutiques, you won't be short of options. See p.188 for a full guide to the city's shopping hotspots, including one of the largest malls in the world, The Dubai Mall (p.200).

## 09  Explore Old Dubai

Wander among traditional Arabic windtower houses
in the beautifully restored Bastakiya area (p.82). Stroll
through the city's history at the nearby Dubai Museum
(p.83) and learn about traditional trades at the Heritage
& Diving Village on the banks of the creek (p.83).

# 10  Discover Downtown

Head to Downtown Dubai for trendy cafes, buzzing bars, chic restaurants and scintillating shopping opportunities at Souk Al Bahar (p.193) and The Dubai Mall (p.200). The dancing Dubai Fountain (p.96) is a light, music and water spectacle not to be missed.

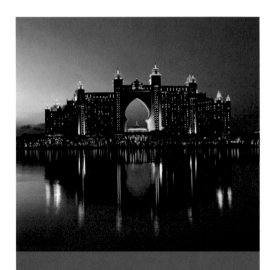

## 11 Life On The Palm

Live the high life on this man-made marvel. Experience the lavish Atlantis hotel with dinner at Nobu (p.269), swim with dolphins (p.115), walk through the watery world of the Lost Chambers (p.115) and take the plunge with the sharks at Aquaventure (p.115).

# 12 Life's A Beach

There's no shortage of sand in Dubai and with kilometres of aquamarine sea beckoning, spending time at the beach is a must. Relax on the golden sands at Jumeirah Beach Park (p.109) or enjoy exclusive facilities at a beachside hotel (p.64).

# Best Of Dubai

## For Adrenaline Junkies

Take a bird's eye view of the growing metropolis while parasailing (p.148) at one of the many beachside hotels or treat yourself to a helicopter tour (p.138).

Dune bashing is a great way to clear the cobwebs and see some spectacular desert vistas. If you go with a tour group (p.139), sand skiing or boarding might be on offer too. If you want to get behind the wheel, you'll find dune buggies and quad biking on the road to Hatta (p.132). If it's too hot then head to Dubai Autodrome (www.dubaiautodrome.com) for a karting race around the 1.2km track or the 500m indoor circuit.

To really get your pulse racing, why not take a dip with the sharks at Dubai Aquarium (p.95)? Novice and experienced divers can take the plunge with the aquarium's 33,000 inhabitants under the supervision of qualified instructors.

## For Big Spenders

Dubai is a shopper's paradise offering everything from market stall haggling to haute couture. If labels are your thing, The Boulevard at Emirates Towers is home to several designers but for anything you can't find there try the exclusive boutiques at Wafi (p.209). Fashionistas will love the collections along Fashion Avenue at The Dubai Mall (p.200) where they can rest their heels at the Armani Cafe post-purchase.

## For Culture Buffs

Delve beneath its glamorous exterior and you'll find the Dubai of old. Sample local cuisine (p.223), hang out in shisha cafes (p.222), explore the souks (p.188), travel on an abra

Fairmont Dubai

(p.63), visit the dhow wharfage on the Deira soide of the Creek, hunt for authentic souvenirs (p.185), and uncover the history at Dubai Museum (p.83). Meanwhile, the art and gallery scene is keeping pace with the skyscrapers. Check out the latest exhibitions at The Third Line (p.127) and The Jam Jar (p.125), or to really immerse yourself in the art world, stay at XVA, a funky gallery and hotel in Bastakiya (p.82).

## For Foodies

Dubai offers an eclectic mix of American fast-food staples, Lebanese street cafes and fine-dining hotel restaurants, but while in town it is the cheap, delicious Arabic food that

should be top of your list. Try shawarmas, falafel, hummus, and tabbouleh, all washed down with the finest fresh juices. See p.223 for the pick of the bunch.

## For Water Babies

From relaxing at the hotel pool and Jumeirah Beach Park (p.109) to diving, snorkelling, sailing and watersports (p.150), there are plenty of opportunities to cool off in the water. Make your own mind up in the battle of the waterparks, choosing between Arabian-themed Wild Wadi (p.116) and Atlantis' hair-raising Aquaventure (p.115).

## For Architecture Admirers

An architect's playground, Dubai is home to many staggering feats of construction. From the sail-shaped Burj Al Arab (p.67) and the pyramidal Raffles hotel (p.69) to the world's tallest building, the Burj Khalifa (p.21), and the teetering towers of Dubai Marina (p.100), there are scores of striking skylines waiting to be captured on camera.

## For Party People

Sip cocktails to a Balearic soundtrack as the sun sinks into the Arabian Gulf at 360° (p.288) or warm up at beach bar favourite Barasti (p.291). Trawl the stylish bars of Souk Al Bahar (p.193), then dance under the stars at open-sky nightclub The Lodge (p.294), or strut your stuff with the designer set at the Cavalli Club (p.64). From the luxurious to the laidback, Dubai's nightlife offerings are surprisingly diverse.

Atmospheric Old Town

# Visiting Dubai

**The UAE warmly welcomes visitors, but has a few rules and regulations that require extra attention. Read on for the vital information.**

## Getting There

Dubai International Airport (DXB) is an important global travel hub, handling more than 37 million passengers in 2008. Currently, more than 130 airlines use the airport, flying to over 220 destinations. 2008 also saw the opening of Terminal 3, which is exclusively used by Emirates, Dubai's rapidly expanding airline. Terminal 1 handles major international airlines, while Terminal 2 is home to newly launched budget operator Fly Dubai. Queues for check-in and departure at Terminals 1 and 2 are bearable, although it can take a while to get through passport control. The airport is clean and modern, facilities are good, and there's a huge duty free section in Terminal 1. The Terminal 3 experience is seamless and stress-free with ample shopping opportunities, spas and chill-out gardens.

### Airport Info

**The main phone number for Dubai International Airport is 04 224 5555. For up-to-date flight information call 04 216 6666 and for baggage services, including lost property, call 04 224 5383.**

# Airport Transfer

If you booked your break through a hotel or travel agency, it's likely that pick-up from the airport will be included. If not, the Metro connects the airport to destinations the length of Dubai (p.54). The Terminal 3 Metro station was the first to open with shuttle services connecting to the other terminals. An airport bus runs to and from the airport every 30 minutes, 24 hours a day. There are a number of loop

| Airlines | | |
|---|---|---|
| Air Arabia | 06 508 8888 | www.airarabia.com |
| Air France | 800 23 823 | www.airfrance.ae |
| American Airlines | 04 393 3234 | www.aa.com |
| British Airways | 800 0441 3322 | www.britishairways.com |
| Emirates | 04 214 4444 | www.emirates.com |
| Etihad Airways | 02 511 0000 | www.etihadairways.com |
| Fly Dubai | 04 301 0800 | www.flydubai.com |
| Gulf Air | 04 271 3222 | www.gulfairco.com |
| KLM Royal Dutch Airlines | 04 602 5444 | www.klm.com |
| Lufthansa | 04 343 2121 | www.lufthansa.com |
| Oman Air | 04 351 8080 | www.oman-air.com |
| Qatar Airways | 04 229 2229 | www.qatarairways.com |
| Royal Brunei Airlines | 04 334 4884 | www.bruneiair.com |
| Royal Jet Group | 02 575 7000 | www.royaljetgroup.com |
| Singapore Airlines | 04 316 6888 | www.singaporeair.com |
| South African Airways | 04 397 0766 | www.flysaa.com |
| United Airlines | 04 316 6942 | www.united.com |
| Virgin Atlantic | 04 406 0600 | www.virgin-atlantic.com |

routes: C1 runs to Satwa, while the C2 goes to Zabeel Park. The fare is Dhs.2.30. Call 800 9090 or log on to http://wojhati. rta.ae to plan your journey.

Taxis leaving from the airport charge an extra Dhs.25 so it costs around Dhs.45 for a journey to the hotels of Sheikh Zayed Road or up to Dhs.90 to Dubai Marina. The stand is straight in front of you as you leave arrivals.

## Visas & Customs

Requirements vary depending on your country of origin. Regulations should be checked before departure. GCC nationals (Bahrain, Kuwait, Qatar, Oman and Saudi Arabia) do not need a visa to enter Dubai. Citizens from many other countries get an automatic visa upon arrival at the airport (see info box below, for the full list). The entry visa is valid for

### Visa On Arrival

Citizens of the following countries receive an automatic visa on arrival: Andorra, Australia, Austria, Belgium, Brunei, Canada, Cyprus, Denmark, Finland, France, Germany, Greece, Hong Kong, Iceland, Ireland, Italy, Japan, Liechtenstein, Luxembourg, Malaysia, Malta, Monaco, Netherlands, New Zealand, Norway, Portugal, San Marino, Singapore, South Korea, Spain, Sweden, Switzerland, United Kingdom, United States of America and Vatican City.

60 days, although you can renew for a further 30 days. For those travelling onwards to a destination other than that of the original departure, a special transit visa (up to 96 hours) may be obtained free of charge through selected airlines.

Certain medications, including codeine, Temazepam and Prozac, are banned even though they are freely available in other countries. High-profile cases have highlighted the UAE's zero tolerance to drugs. Even a miniscule quantity in your possession could result in a lengthy jail term. Bags will also be scanned to ensure you have no offending magazines or DVDs.

## Dos & Don'ts

The UAE is one of the most tolerant and liberal states in the region, but as a guest in a Muslim country you should act accordingly. Lewd and drunken behaviour is not only disrespectful but can lead to arrest and detention. There is also zero tolerance to drinking and driving (p.41). Women should be aware that revealing clothing can attract unwanted attention, so very short skirts and strapless tops should be avoided. Malls have recently put up signs making it clear that inappropriate clothing and public displays of affection are not allowed. It is courteous to ask permission before photographing people, particularly women. With prices for cigarettes low, smoking is very common. However, new laws have banned lighting up in malls and some restaurants so it's best to check the policy before striking up.

Local Knowledge

# Climate

Dubai has a subtropical and arid climate. Sunny blue skies and high temperatures can be expected most of the year. Rainfall is infrequent, averaging only 25 days per year, mainly in winter (December to March). Summer temperatures can hit a soaring 48°C (118°F) and with humidity well above 60% it can make for uncomfortable conditions from June to September. The most pleasant time to visit Dubai is during the cooler winter months when average temperatures range between 30°C and 14°C, perfect for comfortable days on the beach and long, lingering evenings outside. For up-to-date weather forecasts, see www.dubaiairport.com/dubaimet.

# Crime & Safety

Pickpocketing and crimes against tourists are a rarity in Dubai, and visitors can enjoy feeling safe and unthreatened in most places around town. A healthy degree of caution should still be exercised, however, and all hotels offer safes for keeping your valuables and travel documents locked away.

To avoid a great deal of hassle if your personal documents go missing, make sure you keep one photocopy with friends or family back home and one copy in your hotel safe. Dubai Police (p.42) will advise you on a course of action in the case of a loss or theft. If you've lost something in a taxi, call the relevant taxi company (p.60). If you lose your passport, your next stop should be your embassy or consulate (see pull-out map). With high accident rates, extra caution should be taken on Dubai's roads, whether navigating the streets on foot or in a vehicle. Use designated pedestrian crossings wherever possible (jaywalking is actually illegal), and make sure all cars are going to stop before you cross. For more info on road safety, see p.58.

There is zero tolerance towards drink driving, even after one pint, and if you're caught you can expect a spell in prison. With thousands of low-fare taxis available there is no excuse or need.

# Electricity & Water

The electricity supply is 220/240 volts and 50 cycles. Most hotel rooms and villas use the three-pin plug that is used in the UK. Adaptors are widely available and only cost a few dirhams. Tap water is desalinated sea water and is perfectly safe to drink although most people choose mineral water because it tastes better. Bottled water is cheap, especially

| Useful Numbers | |
| --- | --- |
| Police | 999 |
| Ambulance | 998/999 |
| Fire | 997 |
| Department for Tourist Security | 800 4438 |
| Life Pharmacy (24 Hour) | 04 344 1122 |
| Taxi | 04 208 0808 |
| Dubai Airport | 04 224 5555 |
| Flight Information | 04 216 6666 |
| Baggage Services(Lost Property) | 04 224 5383 |
| Weather Updates | 04 216 2218 |
| Directory Enquiries | 181/199 |
| UAE Country Code | 00 971 |

local brands such as Masafi. Bottled water, both local and imported, is served in hotels and restaurants.

# Money

Credit and debit cards are widely accepted around Dubai. Foreign currencies and travellers' cheques can be exchanged in licensed exchange offices, banks and hotels (as usual, a passport is required for exchanging travellers' cheques). Cash is preferred in the souks, markets and in smaller shops, and paying in cash will help your bargaining power. If you've hired a car, be aware that only cash is accepted at petrol pumps.

The monetary unit is the dirham (Dhs.), which is divided into 100 fils. The currency is also referred to as AED (Arab Emirate dirham). Notes come in denominations of Dhs.5 (brown), Dhs.10 (green), Dhs.20 (light blue), Dhs.50 (purple), Dhs.100 (pink), Dhs.200 (yellowy-brown), Dhs.500 (blue) and Dhs.1,000 (browny-purple). The denominations are indicated on the notes in both Arabic and English.

## Police

Dubai Police's Department for Tourist Security is a helpful, friendly service should you run in to any trouble during your stay. For assistance, call the toll free number (800 4438) or visit the Dubai Police website, www.dubaipolice.gov.ae. There's a separate hotline for reporting problems on the beach, including sexual harassment or annoyance by quad bikes (04 203 6398). For other emergency services call 999 for police or ambulance and 997 for fire.

The dirham has been pegged to the US dollar since 1980, at a mid rate of $1 to Dhs.3.6725.

# Language

Arabic is the official language of the UAE, although English, Hindi, Malayalam and Urdu are commonly spoken. Most road signs, shop signs and restaurant menus are in English and

## Basic Arabic

### General

| Yes | na'am |
|---|---|
| No | la |
| Please | min fadlak (m)/min fadliki (f) |
| Thank you | shukran |
| Praise be to God | al-hamdu l-illah |
| God willing | in shaa'a l-laah |

### Greetings

| Greeting (peace be upon you) | as-salaamu alaykom |
|---|---|
| Greeting (in reply) | wa alaykom is salaam |
| Good morning | sabah il-khayr |
| Good morning (in reply) | sabah in-nuwr |
| Good evening | masa il-khayr |
| Good evening (in reply) | masa in-nuwr |
| Hello | marhaba |
| Hello (in reply) | marhabtayn |
| How are you? | kayf haalak (m)/kayf haalik (f) |
| Fine, thank you | zayn, shukran (m)/zayna, shukran (f) |

| Welcome | ahlan wa sahlan |
|---|---|
| Goodbye | ma is-salaama |

## Introduction

| My name is... | ismiy... |
|---|---|
| What is your name? | shuw ismak (m) / shuw ismik (f) |
| Where are you from? | min wayn inta (m) / min wayn (f) |

## Questions

| How many / much? | kam? |
|---|---|
| Where? | wayn? |
| When? | mataa? |
| Which? | ayy? |
| How? | kayf? |
| What? | shuw? |
| Why? | laysh? |
| And | wa |

## Numbers

| Zero | sifr |
|---|---|
| One | waahad |
| Two | ithnayn |
| Three | thalatha |
| Four | arba'a |
| Five | khamsa |
| Six | sitta |
| Seven | saba'a |
| Eight | thamaanya |
| Nine | tiss'a |
| Ten | ashara |

Arabic. The further out of town you go, the more you will find just Arabic, both spoken and on street and shop signs. Arabic isn't the easiest language to pick up, or to pronounce. But if you can throw in a couple of words here and there, you're likely to receive a smile – even if your pronunciation is terrible.

## People With Disabilities

Dubai is starting to consider the needs of visitors with special needs more seriously although, in general, facilities are limited, particularly at older tourist attractions. When asking if a location has wheelchair access, make sure it really does – an escalator is considered 'wheelchair access' by some. That said, Dubai International Airport is well equipped for travellers with special needs, with automatic doors, large lifts and all counters accessible by wheelchair users, as well as several services such as porters, special transportation and quick check-in to avoid long queues. Dubai Transport has a few specially modified taxis for journeys from the airport and around town, and all Metro stations are designed to give easy access to wheelchair users. Metro stations also have tactile floor routes for visually impaired people. Most of the newer malls have wheelchair access and five-star and recently built hotels should offer accessible rooms for visitors with special needs.

## Public Toilets

You will find plenty of clean, modern, western-style toilets in the malls but there is a distinct lack of public bathrooms on shopping streets. Facilities on open beaches tend to be pretty basic, so carrying tissues will come in handy.

# Telephone & Internet

It is possible to buy temporary (three month) SIM cards for mobile phones that work on a pay-as-you go basis. You can buy the package from Du online (www.du.ae) or at its outlets in most malls. For Dhs.55 you will get a welcome bonus of Dhs.20, usage bonus of Dhs.100, and lifetime validity. Etisalat's 'Ahlan' package costs Dhs.60. This includes Dhs.25 credit, and lasts for 90 days with an extra 30 day grace period when you can receive calls. It is available from the airport and malls. You can easily buy top-up cards for both packages from supermarkets, newsagents and petrol stations. Mobile phone numbers in the UAE begin with a prefix of 050, 056 (Etisalat), or 055 (Du).

Wi-Fi is available in many hotel rooms. Most five-star accommodation also includes the use of a business centre (sometimes for a fee) where there are computers and internet access. Many cafes around Dubai offer free Wi-Fi and current hotspots include More cafe, Starbucks, Caribou Coffee and cafes in Mall of the Emirates (p.203) and The Dubai Mall (p.200).

# Time

The UAE is four hours ahead of UTC (Universal Coordinated Time – formerly known as GMT). There is no altering of clocks for daylight saving in the summer, so when Europe and North America lose an hour, the time in the UAE stays the same. Most offices and schools are closed on Fridays (the holy day) and Saturdays. This causes few problems for visitors but be aware that the Metro and some shops don't open until later on Fridays.

Deira Creekside

# Tipping

Tipping practices are similar across hotels, restaurants and bars in Dubai, with tips being shared between all of the staff. Many places add a service charge onto the bill but no one really knows if this actually goes to the staff so many people add a little extra. The usual amount to tip is 10%. Most restaurant bills in hotels should automatically come with 10% municipality tax and 10% service charge included, so check the bill carefully. In a taxi it is standard, but not compulsory, to round up the fare to the nearest Dhs.5.

## Media & Further Reading

# Newspapers & Magazines

There are several English language newspapers in Dubai. You will see free copies of *7Days* on display. This daily tabloid contains international news alongside cinema listings and gossip. *The National* (Dhs.2), *Khaleej Times* and *Gulf News* (both Dhs.3) are broadsheets that offer local and international current affairs with regular supplements. The UK broadsheet, *The Times*, publishes an international edition, and is available daily for Dhs.7 in most supermarkets.

*Live Work Explore* is Explorer Publishing's a monthly lifestyle magazine for expats. It lists upcoming events, gives the low-down on working and living in Dubai and spills the secrets on different areas of the city. You can purchase a copy for Dhs.10 in most of the major shopping malls.

Many of the major glossy magazines are available in Dubai, but if they're imported from the US or Europe, you

## More Info?

If you want to find out more about what's going on in Dubai, check out www.explorerpublishing.com for event listings and the Explorer community forum. If you want to get out of the city on your visit, pick up a copy of *Weekend Breaks Oman & the UAE* for the low-down on the region's best hotels. The *UAE Off-Road Explorer* is essential reading if you fancy getting behind the wheel to explore the country, and *UAE Road Map* will help you find your way back.

can expect to pay at least twice the normal cover price. Alternatively, you can pick up the Middle East versions of popular titles including *Harper's Bazaar, Grazia, OK!* and *Hello!* where you'll find all the regular gossip and news, with extras from around the region.

All international titles are examined and, where necessary, censored to ensure that they don't offend the country's moral codes.

## Television

Most hotel rooms will have satellite or cable, broadcasting a mix of local and international channels. You'll find MTV, major news stations and some BBC programming, in addition to the standard hotel room information loop. For a slice of local flavour, check out local stations City7, Dubai TV and Dubai One, all of which broadcast Arabic soap operas, talks shows and American sitcoms in addition to local news programmes.

## Radio

Catering for Dubai's multinational inhabitants, there are stations broadcasting in English, French, Hindi, Malayalam and Urdu. Daily schedules can be found in newspapers. Of the English-speaking stations, there is a good range to choose from. Tune into Dubai 92 (92.0 FM), Radio 1 (104.1 FM), Radio 2 (99.3 FM), The Coast (103.2) and Virgin Radio (104.4 FM) for music or Dubai Eye (103.8 FM) for talk radio and sport. All stations broadcast regular news and travel updates. You can pick up BBC World Service in English and Arabic (87.9 FM).

# Public Holidays

The Islamic calendar starts from the year 622AD, the year of Prophet Muhammad's migration (Hijra) from Mecca to Al Madinah. Hence the Islamic year is called the Hijri year and dates are followed by AH (AH stands for Anno Hegirae, meaning 'after the year of the Hijra'). As some holidays are based on the sighting of the moon and do not have fixed dates on the Hijri calendar, Islamic holidays are more often than not confirmed less than 24 hours in advance.

The main Muslim festivals are Eid Al Fitr (the festival of the breaking of the fast, which marks the end of Ramadan) and Eid Al Adha (the festival of the sacrifice, which marks the end of the pilgrimage to Mecca). Mawlid Al Nabee is the holiday celebrating the Prophet Muhammad's birthday, and Lailat Al Mi'raj celebrates the Prophet's ascension into heaven.

In general, public holidays are unlikely to disrupt a visit to Dubai, except that shops may open a bit later. During Ramadan however, food and beverages cannot be consumed

## Public Holidays

| | |
|---|---|
| UAE National Day 2010 | Dec 2 (Fixed) |
| Islamic New Year's Day | Dec 7 (Moon) |
| New Year's Day 2011 | Jan 1 (Fixed) |
| Mawlid Al Nabee | Feb 15 (Moon) |
| Lailat Al Mi'raj | Jun 28 (Moon) |
| Eid Al Fitr (3 days) | Aug 30 Moon) |
| Eid Al Adha (4 days) | Nov 6 (Moon) |

in public during the day and smoking and chewing gum is prohibited. These rules apply to Muslims and non-Muslims alike. Women should dress more conservatively and you'll find nightlife dies down for the month.

# Annual Events

Throughout the year the UAE hosts an impressive array of events, from the world's richest horse race and international tennis to well-respected jazz and film festivals. Many attract thousands of international visitors and tickets sell out quickly.

### Dubai Shopping Festival
January to February
Various Locations
www.mydsf.com

Dubai Shopping Festival is a great time to be in the city with bargains galore for shoppers and entertainers, prize draws and kids' shows held in participating malls.

### Dubai Desert Classic
February
Emirates Golf Club
www.dubaidesertclassic.com

A longstanding PGA European Tour fixture and a highly popular event among Dubai's expat golfing community.

### Dubai International Jazz Festival
February
Dubai Media City
www.dubaijazzfest.com

The Jazz Festival attracts a broad range of artists from all around the world to a chilled and pleasant setting in Dubai Media City. Courtney Pine, John Legend, James Blunt and David Gray have all taken to the stage in previous years.

### Dubai Tennis Championships February

The Aviation Club   www.dubaitennischampionships.com
Firmly established on the ATP and WTP circuit, this $1,000,000 tournament attracts the world's top men's and women's seeds.

### Abu Dhabi Desert Challenge March

Empty Quarter, Abu Dhabi   www.uaedesertchallenge.com
This high profile motorsport event attracts some of the world's top rally drivers and bike riders to race Abu Dhabi emirate's challenging desert routes.

### Dubai World Cup March

Meydan Racecourse, Meydan City   www.dubaiworldcup.com
The buzzing atmosphere at the richest horse race in the world (last year's total prize money was more than $20 million), makes it one of the year's big social occasions.

### Camel Racing October to April

Meydan Racecourse, Nad Al Sheba
This popular local sport is serious business with racing camels changing hands for as much as Dhs.10 million. Races take place during winter from 07:00 to 08:30. Admission is free.

### Formula 1 Etihad Airways
### Abu Dhabi Grand Prix November

Yas Marina Circuit, Abu Dhabi   www.yasmarinacircuit.com
The newest fixture on the F1 racing calendar is held only 90 minutes away from Dubai. Abu Dhabi put on a great show in 2009 with a fanzone in the city and live music.

### Dubai World Championship
November

Jumeirah Golf Estates    www.dubaiworldchampionship.com

The final fixture of the Race To Dubai tournament in which the world's best have a shot at a share of the $7.5 million prize fund.

### Dubai International Film Festival
December

Various Locations    www.dubaifilmfest.com

A showcase of Hollywood, international and regional films with screenings in cinemas across the city.

### Dubai Rugby Sevens
December

The Sevens, Al Ain Rd    www.dubairugby7s.com

Over 130,000 people come to watch top international and local Gulf teams battle it out. With friendly rivalry and prizes for fancy dress, the party carries on until the small hours.

### Seeing Stars

The live music scene is looking up in Dubai. A number of large-scale, concerts are hosted each year with megastars such as Kylie, Kanye West and The Backstreet Boys making recent appearances. Other live music fixtures have seen Ian Brown, Paul Weller, The Charlatans and Maroon 5 strut their stuff in recent months, while superstar DJs Fat Boy Slim, Paul Oakenfold, Bob Sinclair and 2ManyDJs have taken to the decks. Up the road in Abu Dhabi, The Killers, Justin Timberlake, Coldplay, Elton John, Shakira and George Michael are just some of acts to grace the stage at Emirates Palace. Check out www.explorerpublishing.com to find out what's happening while you're in town.

# Getting Around

With a brand new Metro system, air-conditioned buses and cheap taxis, travelling round Dubai is easier than you think.

You may have heard horror stories about arduous commutes, sticky strolls in the summer and terrifying taxi journeys but it is surprisingly simple, and pretty cheap, to get around Dubai. Public transport took its first real leap forward in 2009 with the launch of Dubai Metro. Cheap and plentiful taxis are still a popular method of transport, but don't overlook the even cheaper bus routes; it's even possible to explore some areas on foot during the cooler winter months. If you prefer to be in control then hiring a car is a great way to get out of the city but bear in mind the variable driving standards of many motorists. If you're keen to get off the road then take a trip on a traditional abra or modern water bus. Many people use them for daily trips and they offer a fresh perspective on the city.

## Metro

The Dhs.28 billion Dubai Metro opened in September 2009 bringing public transport to the masses. At launch, only 10 of 29 stations of the Red Line were open, with the rest due to follow by end of 2010. The Red Line runs from Rashidiya to the airport, and down Sheikh Zayed Road, terminating at Jebel Ali (see pull-out map). The Green Line, running from Al Qusais on the Sharjah border to Jaddaf, is due to open in August

Crossing the creek by abra

2011, with Purple and Blue lines slated for 2012 and 2014 respectively. Trains run from around 06:00 to 23:00 everyday except Friday (14:00 to 24:00) at intervals of 3 to 4 minutes at peak times. Each train has a section for women and children only, and a first or 'Gold' class cabin. The fare structure operates as a pay-as-you-go system in which you touch your prepaid 'Nol' card in and out at stations (see right).

At the time of writing, the limited number of stations open means that the Metro is more of a must-do experience than a viable means of getting around the city. Most journeys, except those between stations located at major attractions such as Mall of the Emirates and Burj Khalifa, involve connections with feeder buses which run from stations to local areas. Once the rest of the Red Line stations and the Green Line open the Metro's connectivity should improve considerably. In the meantime, check the RTA's journey planner (see right) for travel options or if you are sort for time, it may be best to hop in a taxi.

A monorail runs the length of Palm Jumeirah from the Gateway Towers station on the mainland to Atlantis hotel. Trains run daily from 08:00 to 22:00 and cost Dhs.15 for a single fare or Dhs.25 for a return. Work has also begun on a tramline along Al Sufouh Road which will eventually service Dubai Marina, Media City and Knowledge Village, linking to the Metro system and the Palm Monorail.

## Bus

There are currently more than 79 bus routes servicing the main residential and commercial areas of Dubai. The buses and bus shelters are air-conditioned, modern and clean although they can be rather crowded at peak times. Efforts are being made to display better timetables and route plans at bus stops to encourage people to use buses. The main bus stations are near the Gold Souk in Deira and on Al Ghubaiba Road in Bur Dubai. Buses run at regular intervals until around midnight and a handful of Nightliner buses operate from 23:30 till 06:00. The front three rows of seats on all buses are reserved for women and children only. Cash is not accepted so you need to purchase a Nol card (see below) before boarding. Call the RTA (800 9090) or check the website (www.rta.ae) for comprehensive route plans, timetables and fares.

## Nol Card

Introduced with the opening of the Metro, Nol cards are convenient, rechargeable travel cards which can be used to pay for public transport and street car parking in Dubai. Single journeys start at Dhs.2 for up to 3km, rising to Dhs.6.50 for travel across two or more zones. The red Nol card is a paper ticket aimed at tourists and occasional users. It can be charged for up to 10 journeys, but is only valid on one type of transport – bus, Metro or water bus. The silver Nol card

### Journey Planner

The best way to work out your public transport options is to use the Road & Transport Authority's (RTA) online journey planner at http://wojhati.rta.ae (wojhati is Arabic for journey planner). For further assistance, call the RTA on 800 9090.

costs Dhs.20, including Dhs.14 credit. It can be recharged up to Dhs.500 and is a better option if you plan to use different types of public transport or travel extensively while in town. The gold card is identical to the silver, except that holders are charged first class prices (usually double the standard fare) and can travel in the Gold Class cabins of the Metro. Nol cards can be purchased and topped up at Metro and bus stations and at selected stores including Carrefour and Spinneys.

## Cycling

A lot of care is needed when cycling in the UAE as some drivers pay little attention to other cars, much less cyclists. Also, in the hotter months, you'll be peddling in 45°C heat. If you are visiting in winter and want to cycle, head to Creekside Park (p.121) where you can rent a bike and explore in safety.

## Driving & Car Hire

It's a brave individual who gets behind the wheel in Dubai. Drivers are erratic, roads are constantly changing and the

### Car Rental Agencies

| | | |
|---|---|---|
| **Avis** | 04 295 7121 | www.avisuaecarhire.com |
| **Budget Rent-a-Car** | 04 295 6667 | www.budget-uae.com |
| **Diamond Lease** | 04 343 4330 | www.diamondlease.com |
| **EuroStar Rent-a-Car** | 04 266 1117 | www.eurostarrental.com |
| **Hertz** | 04 282 4422 | www.hertz-uae.com |
| **National Car Rental** | 04 283 2020 | www.national-me.com |
| **Thrifty Car Rental** | 800 4694 | www.thriftyuae.com |

traffic jams can last for hours. On the bright side, most cars are automatic, which makes city driving a lot easier. If you are a confident driver, you'll probably find that driving in Dubai looks much worse than it is in practice. Expect the unexpected and use your mirrors and indicators. Weekends, especially Fridays, are much clearer on the roads but during the week traffic heading into Dubai from Deira in the morning and out in the evening is horrendous. Driving is on the right hand side of the road.

International car rental companies, plus a few local firms, can be found in Dubai. Prices range from Dhs.80 a day for smaller cars to Dhs.1,000 for limousines. Comprehensive insurance is essential; make sure that it includes personal accident coverage. To rent a car, you are required to produce a copy of your passport, a valid international driving licence and a credit card. The rental company may be able to help arrange international or temporary local licences for visitors. Parking is plentiful at most malls and is free for at least the first three hours. Street parking spaces can be hard to find but cost just Dhs.1 for one hour. You can pay in cash or using a Nol card at ticket machines, or those with a local SIM (p.46) can pay via SMS. Instructions are posted on ticket machines.

# Taxi

Until the Metro is fully operational, taxis are likely to remain the most common way of getting around. There are seven companies operating nearly 8,000 metered taxis with a fixed fare structure. All cars are clean and modern, and the fares are cheaper than in most international cities. A fleet of 'ladies'

taxis', with distinctive pink roofs and female drivers, are meant for female passengers and families only. The minimum fare has been raised to Dhs.10 and the pickup charge from the airport is Dhs.25. It is also possible to hire a taxi for 12 or 24 hour periods. Taxis can be flagged down by the side of the road or you can order one through Dubai Transport by calling 04 208 0808. This number is also useful for complaints and lost item inquiries, both of which are usually dealt with promptly. Unlike other cities, there's no 'knowledge' style exam for cabbies here, so it helps to carry a map or the phone number of your destination in case you hail a driver who's new to the city.

# Walking

Most cities in the UAE are very car oriented and not designed to encourage walking. Additionally, summer temperatures of more than 45°C are not conducive to a leisurely stroll. The winter months, however, make walking a pleasant way to explore. There aren't many pavements however, so you're best heading to places such as Al Dhiyafah Road (p.108), Dubai Creek (p.88) and Jumeira Road (p.108) for a wander. There's also a running track along Jumeira Open Beach (p.110), starting from Dubai Marine Resort (www.

**Street Strife**

To make navigation more confusing, places may not always be referred to by their official name. For example, Jumeira Road is often known as Beach Road, and Interchange One on Sheikh Zayed Road is often called Defence Roundabout.

dxbmarine.com), which is popular during the cooler months. Bucking the current trend, Downtown Dubai (p.94) and Dubai Marina are attractive communities designed with pedestrians in mind. Both are interesting places to walk around with plenty of cafes and shops to tempt you off the street.

## Further Out

If you want to explore the UAE during your stay then you'll need a driver or rental car. The East Coast (p.130) is known for its wonderful coastline and watersports, all easily accessible within a two hour drive. There is also a bus service to Abu Dhabi which runs hourly from Al Ghubaiba bus station. The journey takes two hours and costs Dhs.20. Contact the RTA on 800 9090 for more info.

## Water Bus

Opportunities for boat travel in the emirates are limited unless you take a dhow. Crossing the creek by abra is a common method of transport for many people living in Bur Dubai and Deira, with the number of passengers in 2006 estimated at nearly 26 million. It's also a must-do experience while visiting Dubai. Abra stations have been upgraded recently, while fares cost just Dhs.1.

Another recent addition to the creek was a fleet of air-conditioned water buses. These operate on four different routes crossing the creek, with fares set at Dhs.4 per trip. A 'tourist' route also operates, with a 45 minute creek tour costing around Dhs.25 per person.

# Places To Stay

**Nowhere does five-star like Dubai, but while there's a vast array of luxury options to choose from there's also something to suit every budget.**

In addition to a high number of plush hotels, Dubai has plenty of four, three, two and one-star places, self-catering villas, hotel apartments and even a youth hostel. A new hotel seems to spring up every few months – 10,000 additional rooms were planned before the end of 2009. In true 'if you build it, they will come' style, room occupancy rates are amongst the highest in the world. Big discounts are offered to summer visitors when temperatures in Dubai soar.

Most hotels are within 30 minutes of the airport and tend to be either on the beach, by the creek or on Sheikh Zayed Road. The coastal options will probably allow access to a private beach, but if you're in Dubai on business then proximity to the financial and business areas of DIFC and Trade Centre is likely to be a priority. If you are in town to shop then take your pick as malls are everywhere – some with their own hotel. If you're here for a few days, why not combine your city stay with a night at a desert resort, such as Bab Al Shams (p.70)?

## The VIP Set

**With Roberto Cavalli's Cavalli Club (www.cavalliclub. com) at the Fairmont and an Armani Hotel opening at Burj Khalifa (www. armanihotels.com), there are plenty of places to show off your designer threads.**

## *Bonnington*
### JUMEIRAH LAKES TOWERS

## *Perceive Perfection*

The Bonnington boasts 208 non-smoking deluxe rooms and suites, each with spacious en-suite bathroom with freestanding bathtub and rainfall shower. All rooms feature wifi and wired high-speed internet access and large flat screen TVs complete with high-tech connectivity panel and bedside room-control units. The Deluxe Suites come with added touches, such as a separate lounge area with comfortable sofa and a spacious work desk.

Bonnington Jumeirah Lakes Towers PO Box 37246, Dubai
Phone: +971 4 3560000, Fax: +971 4 3560400
Email: reservations@bonningtontower.com
WWW.BONNINGTONTOWER.COM

Image Courtesy of Emaar Properties

### The Address Downtown Dubai

www.theaddress.com

04 436 8888

This luxury hotel has a range of excellent restaurants and one of the coolest bars in the city, Neos (p.299). It has two sister hotels at The Dubai Mall (04 438 8888, map 3 B2) and Dubai Marina (04 436 7777, map 2 A2).

**Map** 3 B3  **Metro** Burj Khalifa/Dubai Mall

### Armani Hotel Dubai

www.dubai.armanihotels.com

04 888 3888

Oozing style and extravagance, the Armani Hotel occupies six floors of the Burj Khalifa and has 160 exquisite rooms and suites. There are four restaurants, an opulent bar and a chic spa.

**Map** 3 B3  **Metro** Burj Khalifa/Dubai Mall

### Atlantis The Palm

www.atlantisthepalm.com

04 426 0000

Situated on the crescent of Palm Jumeirah, the sugary pink Atlantis hotel is a striking landmark. It offers 1,539 rooms including The Lost Chambers Suites which feature floor to ceiling windows looking into the aquarium.

**Map** 1 D1  **Metro** Nakheel

### Bonnington Jumeirah Lakes Towers

www.bonningtontower.com
04 356 0000
In easy reach of Dubai Marina, the five-star Bonnington offers a mix of luxurious guest rooms, suites and serviced residences, plus great leisure, dining and business facilities.
**Map** 2 A2 **Metro** Jumeirah Lake Towers

### Burj Al Arab

www.jumeirah.com
04 301 7777
Architecturally unique, one of the world's tallest hotels stands 321 metres high on a man-made island, and is dramatic, lavish and exclusive. Guests are looked after by a host of butlers. Reservations are essential for dining.
**Map** 2 D1 **Metro** Mall Of The Emirates

### Dubai Festival City

www.ichotelsgroup.com
DFC has two hotels to choose from. The InterContinental (04 701 1111) has extensive spa facilities and great views from all of its rooms and suites; next door is the five-star Crowne Plaza (04 701 2222) with the popular Belgian Beer Cafe (p.291).
**Map** 1 Q7 **Metro** Emirates

### Jumeirah Beach Hotel
www.jumeirah.com
04 348 0000
One of Dubai's key landmarks. Built in the shape of a wave with a colourful interior, the hotel has 598 rooms, all with a sea view. It has several bars and restaurants, including Villa Beach (p.285) and 360° (p.288).
**Map** 2 D1 **Metro** Mall Of The Emirates

### Madinat Jumeirah
www.jumeirah.com
04 366 8888
This resort has two hotels, Al Qasr and Mina A'Salam, with 940 luxurious rooms and suites, and exclusive summer houses, all linked by man-made waterways. Between the hotels is Souk Madinat Jumeirah (p.193).
**Map** 2 D1 **Metro** Mall Of The Emirates

### One&Only Royal Mirage
www.oneandonlyresorts.com
04 399 9999
Blessed with an intimate atmosphere, this hotel features unparalleled service and dining, while a luxury spa treatment here is pure indulgence. Try Moroccan cuisine at Tagine (p.280), or enjoy late nights at Kasbar.
**Map** 2 B1 **Metro** Nakheel

### The Palace – The Old Town

www.thepalace-dubai.com
04 428 7888
Situated close to Burj Khalifa, The Palace boasts 242 deluxe rooms. There's a butler service for all rooms, and views of the world's tallest building. Its Asado (p.245) steak restaurant is recommended.
**Map** 3 B2  **Metro** Burj Khalifa/Dubai Mall

### Park Hyatt Dubai

www.dubai.park.hyatt.com
04 602 1234
Mediterranean and Moorish in style, the Park Hyatt has 225 rooms, each with a balcony or terrace with great views. Its has a prime waterfront location next to Dubai Creek Golf & Yacht Club (p.145).
**Map** 5 C7  **Metro** GGICO

### Raffles Dubai

www.raffles.com
04 324 8888
Raffles has 248 guest rooms and suites and the Raffles Amrita Spa with a unique rooftop garden: an oasis of exotic flowers around a pool. There are nine restaurants and bars; New Asia Bar is a hot nightspot.
**Map** 5 A7  **Metro** Healthcare City

# Destination Hotels

## Al Maha Desert Resort & Spa
04 832 9900
Dubai-Al Ain Rd            www.al-maha.com

Set in 225 square kilometres of desert, the Al Maha resort, accessible only by a 4WD vehicle driven by your own field guide, is congruously set on the slopes of a rising dune and styled as a Bedouin camp. Wild Arabian oryx (maha) wander the resort, and each guest room is a stand-alone property, designed to resemble a traditional Bedouin tent. Surrounded by colourful private gardens, and accessed by chauffeur-driven golf buggy, every one of the 42 suites features a private terrace and infinity plunge pool. The living area is surrounded by panoramic windows that look out over the desertscape, and doors that open on to the patio area. You can opt to dine in private on your patio or at Al Diwaan all-day dining restaurant; the choice is varied and there is a great wine list. The Timeless Spa offers the full range of pampering and there are several activities you can take part in. One of the most popular is a sunset camel ride and champagne toast on the dunes. Other options include a falconry display, horse riding, dune safaris, nature walks and archery.  **Map** 1 L11

## Bab Al Shams Desert Resort & Spa
04 809 6100
Nr Endurance Village      www.jumeirahbabalshams.com

Like a desert mirage come to life, Bab Al Shams is a Bedouin fantasy escape. On approach, bamboo torches guide you to the low-rise building that blends into the imposing dunes that surround it. The rooms, although luxurious, have been designed to evoke a feeling of Bedouin living; bathrooms are similarly designed, and feature clay pots, rustic tones and a large bath that looks like it could have been carved from the earth. Camel rides on the sand dunes are offered to guests, or you can chill out in one of the outdoor holistic swimming pools. The view from the infinity pool leads out into the sand dunes and there is an in-pool bar. Take the pampering up a notch by heading to the Satori Spa.

As the evening sets in, Al Sarab Rooftop Lounge offers shisha and drinks. Al Forsan restaurant serves an international buffet for breakfast, lunch and dinner, but the highlight is Al Hadheerah, which offers a full-on Arabian experience, including a huge buffet, horse and camel displays, belly dancing and traditional music.

**Map** 1 E11

### Kempinski Hotel Mall Of The Emirates  04 341 0000
Al Barsha                                        www.kempinski-dubai.com

As you step into the Kempinski's lobby or one of the excellent restaurants, the world of the mall falls away. The spacious, luxuriously decked out rooms are perfect for families and for business travellers looking for a working base. The fact that guests can walk seamlessly from the hotel to hundreds of outlets, take snowboarding lessons on a real snow ski slope, catch a flick at a 14 screen cinema or drop the kids off for hours of entertainment at Magic Planet amusement centre adds to the all-round attraction of this destination hotel. For the ultimate stay, check into one of the exclusive ski chalets, remove your snow boots, put your feet up by the (fake) fire and tuck into an après-ski afternoon tea with a view of Ski Dubai (p.152). **Map** 2 D2 **Metro** Mall Of The Emirates

### XVA Art Hotel                                04 353 5383
Bastakiya, Bur Dubai                             www.xvagallery.com

This chic boutique hotel manages to maintain Dubai's swanky style, but its rooms have simple, modern edge. The hotel is located in a majlis style building with walkways and archways that fit in with its Bastakiya (p.82) location – one of the oldest heritage sites in the region. The hotel has seven air-conditioned rooms with ensuite bathrooms. Within the compound is the XVA Gallery (p.85), which holds a interesting selection of contemporary art, and there is also a great cafe and a small boutique. As the hotel is in walking distance of 'old Dubai', the busy creek and vibrant souks, a stay here offers a more individual view of Dubai. **Map** 5 B2 **Metro** Al Fahidi

# Other Hotels

## Sheikh Zayed Road

With easy access to Dubai's financial centre and tourist attractions such as The Dubai Mall and Burj Khalifa, the Sheikh Zayed Road hotels offer a balance of work and play. The glamorous Fairmont Dubai (04 332 5555, www.fairmont.com/dubai) is home to Roberto Cavalli's signature nightspot, Cavalli Club, while Amwaj at the deluxe Shangri-La (04 343 8888, www.shangri-la.com) is a contender for Dubai's best seafood restaurant. The Dusit Thani (04 343 3333, www.dusit.com) lives up to its Thai ownership, housing the excellent Thai restaurant Benjarong. For a more intimate stay, the four-star Al Manzil (04 428 5888, www.almanzilhotel.com), in nearby Downtown, features an atmospheric Arabic courtyard restaurant. Further along Sheikh Zayed Road, a Pullman hotel is set to open its doors at Mall of the Emirates (www.pullmanhotels.com).

## Dubai Marina

With sea views, swimming pools and private beaches, sun worshippers are spoilt for choice in Dubai Marina. The new Address Dubai Marina (04 436 7777, www.theaddress.com) has 200 stylish rooms and a fantastic bar, Shades, with views over the marina. The Habtoor Grand Resort & Spa (04 399 5000, www.grandjumeirah.habtoorhotels.com) offers 446 beautiful rooms and suites with views of the Arabian Gulf or the hotel's tropical gardens. Dubai Marriott Harbour Hotel & Suites (04 319 4000, www.marriott.com) has 232 spacious suites, each with its own kitchen and well-stocked bathroom;

The Observatory (p.269) is recommended if cooking is too much trouble. Grosvenor House (04 399 8888, www.grosvenorhouse-dubai.com) is a Starwood hotel with 12 bars and restaurants to choose from, including celebrity Gary Rhodes' Mezzanine. Right on the beach, The Ritz-Carlton (04 399 4000, www.ritzcarlton.com) may stand low in comparison to the marina towers but it excels in terms of style and service. Afternoon tea in the Lobby Lounge is a must (p.262).

## Near The Airport

In the vicinity of the airport, Le Meridien Dubai (04 217 0000, www.lemeridien-dubai.com) has 383 rooms with Le Meridien's signature luxury standards and excellent facilities. It is home to some of the city's favourite restaurants like the Meridien Village Terrace and Yalumba (p.286), and bars such as The Warehouse (p.303). The nearby Al Bustan Rotana Hotel (04 282 0000, www.rotana.com) is likewise locally renowned for having particularly good restaurants including Blue Elephant (p.250).

## On The Creek

While traffic can get a bit snarled up around Deira, the creekside hotels are ideally located for soaking up old Dubai. The Hilton Dubai Creek (04 227 1111, www.hilton.com) offers ultra-minimalist style and features two renowned restaurants – Glasshouse (p.257) and Gordon Ramsay's Verre (p.284). The Sheraton Dubai Creek Hotel & Towers (04 228 1111, www.sheraton.com/dubai) has a spectacular rainforest lobby, 262 rooms (most with creek views) and excellent restaurants, Asiana (p.246) and Vivaldi (p.285). At the five-star Radisson

Blu Hotel, Dubai Deira Creek (04 222 7171, www.radissonblu.com/hotel-dubaideiracreek) you'll be spoilt for choice; Fish Market (p.256) is particularly recommended.

## Beyond The City

On the fringes of the city, hotels offer a break from the bustle. The Desert Palm Dubai (04 323 8888, www.desertpalm.ae) is so tranquil you'll never want to leave. Guests can choose from suites overlooking polo fields, to private villas with a pool. Signature restaurant Rare (p.274) is a must for meat lovers, while Epicure (p.254) is a gourmet deli. Al Sahra Desert Resort 04 367 9500, www.alsahra.com) is a good base from which to explore the dunes around Dubai, offering desert safaris and activities including kiting, archery and belly dancing lessons.

# Hostels & Guesthouses

The pick of the guesthouses are Fusion (www.fusionhotels.com/bedandbreakfastsindubai.html), which has good facilities including pools, and the XVA Gallery (p.85), which is an inspired guesthouse joined to an art gallery in Bastakiya.

Dubai Youth Hostel (04 298 8161, www.uaeyha.com) offers single, double, triple and dorm rooms starting from Dhs.90. Hotel apartments are great for extended stays; they are often kitted out with top-class facilities and are located across Dubai. The Bonnington Jumeirah Lakes Towers (p.67) has one to three bedroom serviced apartments, as well as hotel suites. Villas are another option for long or short stays; visit www.mydubaistay.com for accommodation in different areas, with online availability, booking and a cost comparison chart.

# Exploring

# Explore Dubai

**From slick city attractions to expansive deserts, Dubai is an emirate of superlatives that will impress even the most seasoned traveller.**

Dubai provides a wealth of contrasting images: Ferraris parked outside falafel shops, massive skyscrapers shading pristine mosques, billionaires, cranes, camels, palaces and windtowers. The city is filled with luxurious five-star hotels and huge shopping malls, it has some of the top nightspots in the Middle East, and is home to a range of museums, heritage sites and places of cultural interest. Quite a mix.

Don't let the traffic and ever-expanding footprint disorient you – Dubai itself is fairly easy to navigate and explore, especially with the introduction of the Metro (p.54). The city runs along the Arabian Gulf coast, and the older sections of the city, such as Deira and Bur Dubai, are situated in the northern end and around the Dubai Creek. From there, the city stretches south along Sheikh Zayed Road towards new developments such as The Palm (p.114) and Dubai Marina (p.73).

Most of the city's historical attractions are located around the creek which, until recently, was the residential and commercial hub of the city. Bastakiya (p.82) and the souks of Deira (p.188) have managed to retain much of the old Dubai character and multiculturalism, with narrow streets selling everything from wholesale grain to traditional Emirati dress.

The bright lights of Deira

These are also the best areas to find a traditional Indian or Arabic meal. Try Saravana Bhavan (p.276) for a spicy south-Indian thali, or Bastakiyah Nights (p.248) for a taste of Emirati machboos.

If large and luxurious better describes the Dubai of your dreams, newer areas like Downtown Dubai (p.94), home to the world's tallest building, and the Dubai Marina (p.73) should be your target destinations. The towering skyscrapers and enormous malls that fill these impressive developments contain some of the best shopping and nightlife in the Middle East. The Dubai Mall (p.200) has nearly 1,200 shops, while the sheer volume of restaurants and bars on the Al Sufouh strip (p.114), The Palm and the Marina could keep you full for years.

# Heritage Sites

# Museums & Art Galleries

# Parks

# Beaches & Beach Parks

# Bastakiya: Old Dubai

**For heritage and a glimpse into Dubai's past, Bastakiya's narrow streets are not to be missed.**

If you're in search of a dose of tradition, step out of the modern world and into a pocket of the city that harks back to a bygone era. The Bastakiya area is one of the oldest heritage sites in Dubai and certainly the most atmospheric. The neighbourhood dates from the early 1900s when traders from the Bastak area of southern Iran were encouraged to settle there by tax concessions granted by Sheikh Maktoum bin Hashar, the ruler of Dubai at the time.

The area is characterised by traditional windtower houses, built around courtyards and clustered together along a winding maze of alleyways. The distinctive four-sided windtowers (barjeel), seen on top of the traditional flat-roofed buildings, were an early form of air conditioning.

There are some excellent cultural establishments in and around Bastakiya, and a short stroll along the creek will bring you to the Textile Souk and abra station, from where you can cross the water to explore the souks on the Deira side (see p.188). You can make a single crossing on a communal abra for Dhs.1, or hire your own (plus driver) for an hour-long tour for Dhs.100.

## Dubai Museum

Nr Bastakiya, Bur Dubai

04 353 1862

www.dubaitourism.ae

Located in and under Al Fahidi Fort, which dates back to 1787, this museum is creative and well thought-out. All parts of life from Dubai's past are represented in an attractive and interesting way; walk through a souk from the 1950s, stroll through an oasis, see into a traditional house, get up close to local wildlife, learn about the archaeological finds or go 'underwater' to discover the pearl diving and fishing industries. There are some entertaining mannequins to pose with too. Entry costs Dhs.3 for adults and Dhs.1 for children under 6 years old. Open daily 08:30 to 20:30 (14:30 to 20:30 on Fridays). **Map** 5 B2 **Metro** Al Fahidi

## Heritage & Diving Village

Nr Al Shindagha Tunnel, Al Shindagha

04 393 7139

www.dubaitourism.ae

Located near the mouth of Dubai Creek, the Heritage & Diving Village focuses on Dubai's maritime past, pearl diving traditions and architecture. Visitors can observe traditional potters and weavers practising their craft the way it has been done for centuries. Local women serve traditionally cooked snacks – one of the rare opportunities you'll have to sample genuine Emirati cuisine. Camel rides are also available most afternoons and evenings. The Village is particularly lively during the Dubai Shopping Festival (p.51) and Eid celebrations, with performances including traditional sword dancing. Open daily 08:30 to 10:00 (Fridays 16:30 to 22:00). **Map** 5 B1 **Metro** Al Ghubaiba

### The Majlis Gallery

04 353 6233

The Bastakiya, Bur Dubai — www.themajlisgallery.com

The Majlis Gallery is a converted Arabian house, complete with windtowers and courtyard. Small, whitewashed rooms lead off the central garden and host exhibitions by contemporary artists. In addition to the fine art collection, there's an extensive range of hand-made glass, pottery, fabrics, frames, and unusual furniture. The gallery hosts exhibitions throughout the year, and is worth visiting at any time. Open Saturday to Thursday, 10:00 to 18:00.
**Map** 5 B2 **Metro** Al Fahidi

### Sheikh Mohammed Centre For Cultural Understanding

04 353 6666

The Bastakiya, Bur Dubai — www.cultures.ae

This facility was established to help visitors and residents understand the customs and traditions of the UAE. It organises tours in Jumeira Mosque (p.109), a walking tour of the Bastakiya area, and weekly coffee mornings where UAE nationals explain the Emirati way of life. The centre is worth a look for the majlis-style rooms around the courtyard and great views through the palm trees and windtowers. Open Sunday to Thursday 09:00 to 19:00. **Map** 5 B3 **Metro** Al Fahidi

### Sheikh Saeed Al Maktoum's House

04 393 7139

Nr Heritage & Diving Village, Al Shindagha

Dating from 1896, this carefully restored house-turned-museum is built in the traditional manner of the Gulf coast, using coral covered in lime and sand-coloured plaster. The

interesting displays in many rooms show rare and wonderful photographs of life in Dubai pre-oil. There is also an old currency and stamp collection, and great views over the creek from the upper floor. Entry is Dhs.2 for adults, Dhs.1 for children and free for children under 6 years old.
**Map** 5 B1 **Metro** Al Ghubaiba

## XVA Gallery
04 353 5383

The Bastakiya, Bur Dubai                                    www.xvagallery.com

Situated in the centre of Bastakiya, this is one of Dubai's most interesting art galleries. Originally a windtower house, it's worth a visit for its architecture alone. The gallery focuses on paintings, sculpture and art installations, and hosts exhibitions throughout the year. It is also a boutique hotel with guest rooms offering views over the minarets to Bur Dubai. Open Saturday to Thursday 09:00 to 19:00. **Map** 5 B2 **Metro** Al Fahidi

## If you only do one thing in...
# Bastakiya

Get schooled at the informative Dubai Museum (p.83). Learn about life in Dubai 50 years ago to really appreciate how much has changed.

## Best for...

**Eating & Drinking:** For an atmospheric evening of Arabian food in a traditional setting, book a table at Bastakiyah Nights (p.248).

**Families:** Let the kids hop on a camel while you gorge on freshly baked bread, all in the middle of living history at the Heritage & Diving Village (p.83).

**Relaxation:** Duck into tranquillity at The Majlis Gallery (p.84) or XVA (p.85).

**Shopping:** A visit to the Textile Souk (p.195) is a memorable affair, and if your haggling skills are up to speed you could take home a pashmina at a bargain price.

**Sightseeing:** The winding alleyways of Bastakiya (p.82) will linger in the memory long after you leave Dubai.

Traditional Arabian architecture

Bastakiya: Old Dubai

# Deira & The Creek: Dubai's Port

Deira's busy streets capture the bustling essence of old Dubai, while the emirate's trading traditions live on at the creek.

Once the residential hub of Dubai, Deira remains an incredibly atmospheric area. Narrow convoluted streets bustle with activity while gold, spices, perfumes and general goods are touted in its numerous souks. Likewise, Dubai Creek, upon which Deira sits, was once the centre of Dubai commerce. Both sides of the creek are lined by corniches that come alive in the evenings as residents head out for a stroll and traders take stock. Take the time to meander along the Deira side of the creek where men in traditional south-Asian garb unload wooden dhows that are docked by the water's edge and are tightly packed with everything from fruit and vegetables to televisions and maybe even a car or two. And no visitor should leave without experiencing a trip across the water on a commuter abra (p.63) for Dhs.1, or a tourist abra (Dhs.100 for an hour's private trip).

Start with a wander through the Textile Souk (p.195) on the Bur Dubai side before taking an abra towards Deira. Once on the Deira side, cross the corniche and head towards the souk district. First stop is the Spice Souk (p.194), where the aroma of saffron and cumin fill the air. Nearby, the streets in and around the Gold Souk (p.190) are filled with shops shimmering with gold and platinum.

If it's rugs you want, then Deira Tower on Al Nasr Square (map 5 C3) is worth a visit. Around 40 shops offer a colourful

Clocktower Roundabout

profusion of carpets from Iran, Pakistan, Turkey and Afghanistan to suit everyone's taste and pocket. For dinner with a view, head to the top of the Hyatt Regency where Al Dawaar (p.243) hosts an incredible buffet within its rotating dining room. Afterwards, go for a stroll along the Gulf-side of Deira corniche. If you're staying on the Deira side of town, Al Mamzar has great section of beach (see below).

### Al Ahmadiya School & Heritage House   04 226 0286
Al Khor St, Al Ras   www.dubaitourism.ae

Established in 1912 for Dubai's elite, Al Ahmadiya School was the earliest regular school in the city. A visit here is an excellent opportunity to see the history of education in the UAE. Situated in what is becoming a small centre for heritage (Al Souk Al Khabeer), it is an interesting example of a traditional Emirati family home, and dates back to 1890. Admission to both is free. Open Saturday to Thursday 07:30 to 19:30 and 14:30 to 19:30 on Friday.  **Map** 5 B2  **Metro** Al Ras

### Al Mamzar Beach Park   04 296 6201
Nr Hamriya Port, Al Mamzar

With its four clean beaches, open spaces and plenty of greenery, Al Mamzar is a popular spot. The well-maintained beaches have sheltered areas for swimming and changing rooms with showers. Air-conditioned chalets, with barbecues, can be rented on a daily basis, costing from Dhs.160 to Dhs.200. There are two swimming pools with lifeguards on duty. Entrance is Dhs.5 per person or Dhs.30 per car (including all occupants).  **Map** 1 R3  **Metro** Al Qiyadah

## Creekside Souks

Deira's three main souks – the Spice Souk, the Fish Souk and the Gold Souk – present some of the best examples of living heritage that Dubai has to offer. Smelly as it may be, an early morning trip through the Fish Souk makes for a great photo opportunity. The Gold Souk (p.190) gets crowded on weekend afternoons, but spend an hour or two here during the week and enjoy a form of window shopping that's very different from a mall experience. For the best insight into the region's varied cuisines, take a walk through the Spice Souk where you'll be bombarded by the colours and smells of spices you've never heard of. Just across the creek on the Bur Dubai side sits the covered Textile Souk (p.195) with its myriad of bright fabrics.  **Map** 5 C2  **Metro** Al Ras

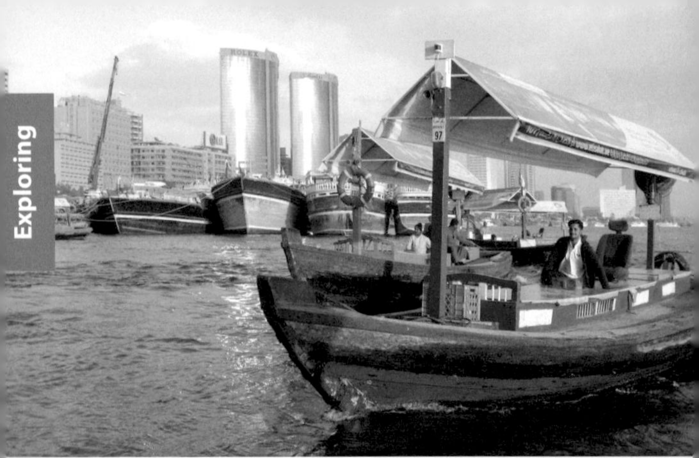
ROLEX
97

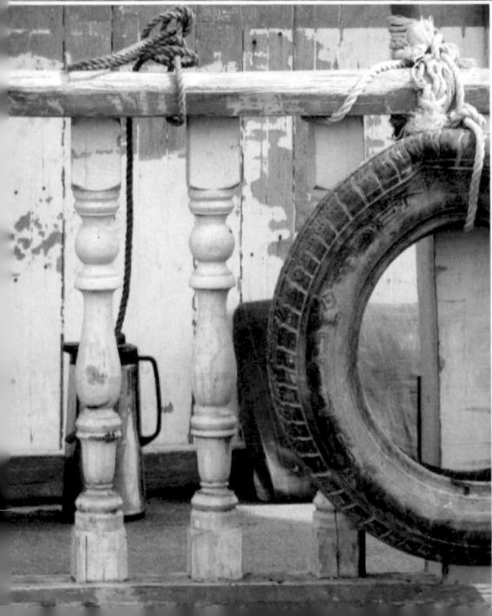

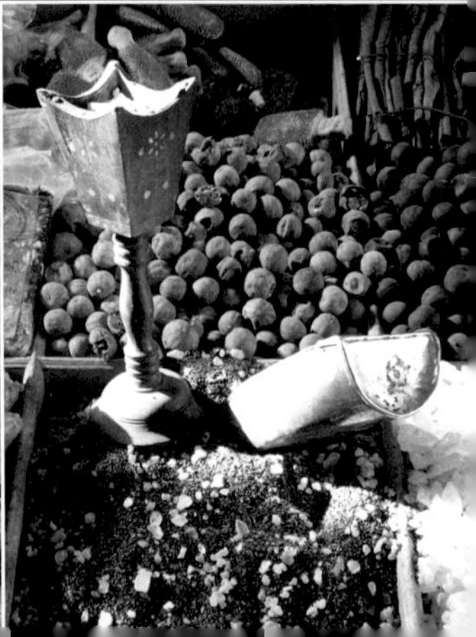

## If you only do one thing in...
# Deira & The Creek

Watch the dhows unload at the corniche, then head for a stroll around Dubai's famous souks.

## Best for...

**Eating & Drinking:** Hop on a dhow for a delicious dinner cruise (p.223). This is by far the best way to get your fill of food, facts, and photographs.

**Families:** Leave the traffic-filled bridges and take the kids across the creek by abra.

**Relaxation:** Step into the calm courtyard of the Al Ahmadiya School & Heritage House (p.90), where you'll find some quiet in the Deira storm.

**Shopping:** Stroll through the glittering streets of the Gold Souk (p.190) before following your nose to the Spice Souk (p.194).

**Sightseeing:** Reserve a table at the Hyatt Regency's Al Dawaar (p.243). The city's only revolving restaurant offers fantastic views of the creek and beyond.

Clockwise from top: an abra on Dubai Creek, Spice Souk, dhow details

**Exploring**

# Downtown & Sheikh Zayed Road

The world's tallest building, Dubai's largest mall and the most photographed skyline in the city are all in Dubai's newest residential area.

The newest place in town to explore, Downtown Dubai is a spectacular mix of shops, restaurants, entertainment and architecture, while nearby is a stretch of Dubai's original stunning skyscraper strip, which lines either side of Sheikh Zayed Road and features some of the city's top hotels and building design. At the heart of Downtown Dubai is the world's tallest tower, the shimmering Burj Khalifa, which points like a needle more than 800m skywards and, when fully opened, will contain apartments, hotels, shops and entertainment facilities. By its base are The Dubai Mall, Old Town, and Dubai Fountain, the development's spectacular centrepiece. The Dubai Mall (p.200) is a huge shopping centre full of top-end retail brands, an array of excellent eateries and some fantastic entertainment options, such as Dubai Aquarium and SEGA Republic. There are two The Address hotels in the area, with the views from the 63rd floor Neos bar (p.299) at The Address Downtown Dubai well worth taking in. Old Town, which is home to the atmospheric Souk Al Bahar (p.193), takes strong influences from traditional Arabia, with windtowers, mosaics, courtyards, passageways and fortress-like finishes, all of which are beautifully lit at night. Other hotels in the Downtown area include The Palace Hotel and

94                                    Dubai Mini **Visitors'** Guide

Al Manzil, which are home to Asado steakhouse (p.245) and upmarket sports bar Nezesaussi (p.299) respectively.

The buzzing strip over on Sheikh Zayed Road is known for the striking architecture of its high-rise residential buildings, office towers and top-class hotels. From the Dubai World Trade Centre to Interchange One (known as Defence Roundabout), the wide, skyscraping 3.5km stretch is the subject of many a photo, as well as after-hours hook-ups in the various happening hotspots. With so many residents, tourists and business people around, this area really buzzes at night, as the crowds flit from restaurants to bars to clubs.

### Dubai Aquarium & Underwater Zoo    04 448 5200
The Dubai Mall,
 Downtown Dubai                www.thedubaiaquarium.com

The Dubai Aquarium is a sight to behold in the middle of The Dubai Mall; through its three storey main viewing panel, the bewildering variety of tropical fish (over 33,000 in total) is displayed to fish fans and passing shoppers free of charge. For a closer view of the main tank's inhabitants, which include fearsome looking but generally friendly sand tiger sharks, you can pay to walk through the 270° viewing tunnel. Also well worth a look is the Underwater Zoo, which has exhibits from the world's waters, and includes residents such as penguins, piranhas and an octopus. If you're feeling adventurous, you can even go for a scuba dive in the tank (call ahead to book). A ticket to the interactive Underwater Zoo and Tunnel Experience costs Dhs.50 (or Dhs.25 for just the tunnel).
**Map** 3 B2 **Metro** Burj Khalifa/Dubai Mall

## Dubai Fountain

Nr Burj Khalifa, Downtown Dubai      www.thedubaimall.com

This spectacular Downtown centrepiece draws crowds to witness the regular evening shows. Designed by the same team that created the famous Bellagio fountains in Las Vegas, the water, light and music combination is a captivating showstopper. Jets of water shoot 150m into the air along the length of the Burj lake in synchronisation with classical and Arabic music, while the Burj Khalifa at night forms a memorable backdrop. The show, which is every 20-30 minutes after sunset, can be viewed from outside The Dubai Mall and Souk Al Bahar, or alternatively take a table at one of the many outdoor restaurants and enjoy several shows as you dine.

**Map** 3 B2  **Metro** Burj Khalifa/Dubai Mall

## Emirates Towers

04 330 0000

Sheikh Zayed Rd, Trade Centre      www.jumeirah.com

These twin towers are a true Dubai landmark. At 350m, the office tower was the tallest building in the Middle East and Europe until the Burj Khalifa surpassed it. The smaller tower, at 305m, houses the Emirates Towers hotel plus many eating and drinking spots. Harry Ghatto's is a city favourite for karaoke, while the cocktails and fancy pub fare at Scarlett's are popular with the after work crowd. For a real thrill, the views from the aptly named 51st floor Vu's Bar (p.285) are superb. If shopping makes your heart beat, The Boulevard is probably Dubai's most exclusive mall.

**Map** 3 D2  **Metro** Emirates Towers

Dubai Fountain & Old Town Island

## SEGA Republic

04 448 8484

The Dubai Mall, Downtown Dubai     www.segarepublic.com

This indoor theme park located in The Dubai Mall offers a range of indoor thrills, courtesy of the nine main attractions and the 200 arcade games. A Power Pass (Dhs.140) gets you all-day access to the big attractions, which include stomach-flipping rides like the Sonic Hopper, the SpinGear and the Halfpipe Canyon. Unlike many other shopping mall amusement centres, SEGA Republic is for all ages, and features some truly unique thrills.

**Map** 3 B2  **Metro** Burj Khalifa/Dubai Mall

## If you only do one thing in...
# Downtown Dubai & Sheikh Zayed Road

Dine alfresco while watching the nightly Dubai Fountain shows (p.96).

## Best for...

**Eating & Drinking:** Japanese restaurant Zuma in DIFC offers possibly one of the best, funkiest, fine-dining experiences in Dubai (p.286).

**Families:** Take the kids to SEGA Republic (p.97) and be amazed at how far technology has come.

**Relaxation:** Take time out at The Spa at The Palace; after a treatment here you'll feel like royalty (p.172).

**Shopping:** With over 1,000 stores, The Dubai Mall is a shopaholic's paradise (p.200).

**Sightseeing:** The panoramic views over Downtown Dubai from the 63rd floor bar Neos (p.299) are priceless.

Clockwise from top: Old Town, Emirates Towers, The Dubai Aquarium

Downtown & Sheikh Zayed Road

# Dubai Marina & JBR: New Dubai

## Head to the Marina for high-rise heaven, a thriving cafe culture and bustling beach action.

Previously home to just a handful of waterfront hotels, the Marina is the epitome of new Dubai's rise to modern prominence. Apartment buildings (finished or still under construction) have sprouted up along every inch of the man-made waterway, while between the marina and the shore is the massive Jumeirah Beach Residence (JBR) development, which now dwarfs the five-star beach resorts such as the Hilton and Ritz-Carlton. The pedestrianised walkways that run around the marina and parallel to the coast have evolved into lively strips of cafes and restaurants, which throng with people in the evenings when the lit-up skyscrapers are at their most impressive. On the water, luxury boats fill the marina's berths, and thrill seekers take to the sea to parasail or waterski.

### JBR Beach
Dubai Marina

At nearly 2km long, this bay of golden sand is massively popular. The spaces in front of the hotels are reserved for guests, but there are plenty of areas in between that fill with families and groups of friends at weekends. The waters are fairly calm here and the shallow areas are scattered with bathers, while the hotels offer a variety of watersports such as parasailing that anyone can sign up for. There is a big carpark, but this gets fairly congested at peak times. **Map** 2 A1 **Metro** Dubai Marina

## Marina Walk

Dubai Marina

The Marina Walk boulevard starts at the base of Dubai Marina Towers and, when completed, will provide continuous pedestrian access around the 11km perimeter of the water. It is home to several independent restaurants and cafes such as popular Lebanese restaurant and shisha spot Chandelier (04 366 3606). It is a great place for a stroll at any time but it really comes to life in the evenings and cooler months when you can sit and gaze out across the rows of yachts and the flashing lights of high-rise hotels and apartments. Further along the walkway, on the same side of the water, is Dubai Marina Mall (p.199), which houses dozens of popular shops and restaurants an Address hotel. Further still is the Dubai Yacht Club, which has the chic bar and restaurant Aquara (04 362 7900).
**Map** 2 A2 **Metro** Dubai Marina

## The Walk

Jumeirah Beach Residence, Dubai Marina

The Walk at JBR is an outdoor parade of shops, restaurants and hotels parallel to the beach and is a huge leisure-time draw for Dubai residents. Strolling from one end to the other of this 1.7km promenade will take you past a whole host of retail and eating options, with the scores of alfresco diners and Saturday strollers providing some excellent people watching. From Wednesday to Saturday the outdoor Covent Garden Market by Rimal court is an added attraction, with street entertainers and craft stalls creating a colourful atmosphere (see p.189). **Map** 2 A1 **Metro** Dubai Marina

## If you only do one thing in...
# Dubai Marina & JBR

Head to the beach for an early morning swim before rewarding yourself with a hearty alfresco breakfast at Le Pain Quotidien on The Walk.

## Best for...

**Eating & Drinking:** Tuck into delicious seafood alfresco at Dubai Marina Yacht Club's Aquara (04 362 7883) and watch Marina life sail by as you dine.

**Families:** Give the family the thrill of a lifetime with a camel ride on JBR Beach.

**Relaxation:** Book a massage at the Timeless Spa (p.174) at the Harbour Hotel then sip cocktails at The Observatory (p.269) for incredible views of the Marina.

**Shopping:** Stroll through the Covent Garden Market (p.189) on The Walk and pick up some works by Dubai's emerging designers and artisans.

**Sightseeing:** Take the hour-long Captain Jack dhow tour (Bristol Middle East, p.139) for some spectacular views of the Marina and JBR from the water.

Developments in Dubai Marina

# Festival City & Garhoud

**Relaxed and refined, Festival City is an oasis of calm in an otherwise rushed metropolis.**

Situated on the creek just down from Deira, Festival City has grown into a massive eating, shopping and entertainment complex. With an open marina, a bowling centre and cinema, a world-class golf course and several restaurants, Festival City has enough attractions to warrant a day of exploring, strolling and window-shopping.

Festival City is bounded at one end by Al Badia Golf Club (p.146) and its gorgeous clubhouse, and on the other by the InterContinental (p.67) and Crowne Plaza (p.67) hotel towers which house the Belgian Beer Café (p.291). In between sits the Festival Waterfront Centre, one of Dubai's more spacious and relaxed shopping malls, as well as an outdoor concert venue that has hosted Paul Weller, Kylie Minogue, Maroon 5 and Queen. A canal-like waterway, complete with tiny passenger boats and alfresco dining options, meanders through the area and is perfect for post-meal, evening strolls. Aside from shopping and dining, Festival City hosts several events throughout the year, including dragonboat races, children's events and fashion shows. Check out www.festivalcentre.com for a schedule of upcoming events.

Nearby in Garhoud, The Aviation Club (04 282 4122, www.aviationclub.ae) houses the Dubai Tennis Stadium, home of the Dubai Tennis Championships. The Irish Village (p.298) is also part of the Aviation Club and has long been an institution on the Dubai drinking scene with live music and several annual events such as the Dubai Sound City music festival. Next door to The Aviation Club sits Century Village, a collection of licensed alfresco restaurants including Sushi Sushi (p.280). A bit closer to Deira is the Dubai Creek Golf & Yacht Club, incorporating the creekside Boardwalk restaurant (p.250) and Park Hyatt Dubai (p.69), home to the lovely Amara Spa (p.165). The club's creekside golf course is one of Dubai's nicer offerings and is open to non-members. The Park Hyatt's popular restaurants, including The Thai Kitchen (p.281), all sit by the creek as well.

If you only do one thing in...

# Festival City & Garhoud

Spend an evening over pints and live music at the Irish Village (p.298), one of the city's oldest and most popular pubs.

## Best for...

**Eating & Drinking:** Enjoy a steaming pot of mussels on the outdoor terrace of The Belgian Beer Café (p.291) while watching the sun go down.

**Families:** The bowling alley in Festival Waterfront Centre (p.198) is a blast for all ages.

**Sightseeing:** The views from Boardwalk (p.250) are some of the best in the city.

**Shopping:** The spacious, well-designed halls of Festival Waterfront Centre (p.198) offer a calmer shopping environment than the busier, larger malls.

**Relaxation:** Indulge yourself with a treatment at the highly rated Amara Spa at the Park Hyatt Dubai (p.69).

Clockwise from top: Dubai Creek Golf & Yacht Club, Dubai Festival City, Boardwalk

# Jumeira: Beachside Life

Jumeira's beaches, boutiques and art galleries offer a pleasant retreat from the city's bustling core.

Jumeira might not have the exotic atmosphere or history of Deira, but its beaches, shopping centres and pleasant, wide roads make up for it. That's not to say it doesn't have any culture. Jumeira Mosque (p.109) is one of the most recognisable places of worship in the city and welcomes tourists with tours and educational programmes, while the many galleries will keep art enthusiasts happy.

Jumeira is one of the most desirable addresses for well-off expats and home to the infamous, coiffeured 'Jumeira Janes' – well-off expat women who can often be found in the boutiques along Jumeira Road and the shops in Mercato (p.204). The popular Jumeira Open Beach (p.110) has showers and lifeguards, but unfortunately attracts a few voyeurs, so you may prefer to try the more private Jumeira Beach Park (p.109).

Just outside Jumeira, on the border with Satwa, lies Al Dhiyafah Street – the main destination for anyone needing to feed their post-club hunger, show off their expensive customised cars, or watch the city pass by as they enjoy some street-side Lebanese fare. If you're out past midnight, don't miss having a bite at either Al Mallah (p.243) or Ravi's (p.274).

## Green Art Gallery

04 344 9888

51st Street, Villa 23, Nr Dubai Zoo,
  Jumeira          www.gagallery.com

Since its founding in 1995, Green Art Gallery has focused
on art from the Arab world. It has acted as a catalyst for
many internationally recognised artists from the Levant and
continues to stay relevant in the growing contemporary
Arabic art scene. With large white minimalist walls and lots
of floor space, Green Art makes a great stop-off if you fancy
some peace, quiet and culture. Seasonal exhibitions are held
throughout the year. **Map** 1 M3 **Metro** Financial Centre

## Jumeira Beach Park

04 349 2111

Jumeira Rd, Jumeira

You get the best of both worlds here with plenty of grassy
areas and vast expanses of beach. The facilities include
sunlounger and parasol hire, lifeguards, toilets, showers,
snack bar, play park and barbecue pits. Entry is Dhs.5 per
person or Dhs.20 per car, including all occupants. Mondays
are for women and children only. Open daily from 07:00,
closing at 22:00 Sunday to Wednesday, and at 22:30 Thursday
to Saturday and on holidays. **Map** 1 K3 **Metro** Business Bay

## Jumeira Mosque

04 353 6666

Jumeira Rd, Jumeira          www.cultures.ae

This is the most beautiful mosque in the city and perhaps the
best known. Non-Muslims are not usually permitted entry
to a mosque, but the Sheikh Mohammed Centre for Cultural

Understanding (p.84) organises weekly tours (Saturday, Sunday, Tuesday and Thursday mornings at 10:00). Visitors are guided around the mosque and told all about the building, and then the hosts give a talk on Islam and the prayer ritual. You must dress conservatively – no shorts and no sleeveless tops. Women must also cover their hair with a head scarf or shawl, and all visitors will be asked to remove their shoes. Cameras are allowed and large groups can book private tours.
**Map** 1 N3 **Metro** Al Jafiliya

## Jumeira Open Beach

Nr Dubai Marine Beach Resort & Spa, Jumeira
One of the most popular free beaches in the city, this clean area offers both showers and lifeguards. Unfortunately, men staring at the sunbathing women can often be found loitering in the area. They may make the scene uncomfortable, but on the whole they mean no harm. A sprung running and bike track runs the length of the beach.
**Map** 1 M3 **Metro** Emirates Towers

## Majlis Ghorfat Um Al Sheif

04 394 6343
www.dubaitourism.ae

Jumeira Rd, Jumeira
Constructed in 1955 from coral stone and gypsum, this simple building was used by the late Sheikh Rashid bin Saeed Al Maktoum as a summer residence. The ground floor is an open veranda, while upstairs the majlis (meeting place) is decorated with carpets, cushions, lanterns and rifles. The Majlis is located just off Jumeira Road on Street 17, beside HSBC bank. Entry is Dhs.1 for adults and free for children

Jumeira Mosque

under 6 years old. It opens at 08:30 and closes at 20:30 every day except Friday, when it opens at 14:30.
**Map** 1 K3 **Metro** Business Bay

## Safa Park

04 349 2111

Al Wasl Rd, Nr Union Co-op & Choithrams, Al Wasl

This huge, artistically divided park is a great place to escape the commotion of nearby Sheikh Zayed Road. Its many sports fields, barbecue sites and play areas make it one of the few places where locals and expats come together. There's a large boating lake in the centre of the park, tennis and basketball courts for the public and a flea market held on the first Saturday of every month. Tuesday is ladies' day, but there is also a permanent ladies' garden within the park. Entry costs Dhs.3 (free for children under 3 years old). There's a great running track around the park's perimeter.
**Map** 3 A1 **Metro** Business Bay

# If you only do one thing in...
# Jumeira

Take a tour of the most beautiful mosque in the city, and one of the few in the country open to non-Muslims.

## Best for...

**Eating & Drinking:** Dine on fantastic Cuban fare while listening to a live Latino band at El Malecon (p.254).

**Families:** Head to Jumeira Beach Park (p.109), rent a sunbed and parasol and experience the Dubai you've seen in the brochures.

**Relaxation:** Feel like a 'Jumeira Jane' by slipping into Elche spa for a treatment (04 349 4942).

**Shopping:** Enjoy a wander through the malls and thriving independent fashion boutiques that line Jumeira Road.

**Sightseeing:** Spend an afternoon at Jumeira Open Beach (p.110) and watch the Burj Al Arab from afar.

Clockwise from top: Jumeira Beach Park, Majlis Ghorfat Um Al Sheef, Mercato

Jumeira: Beachside Life

# The Palm Jumeirah & Al Sufouh

With a modern man-made wonder, world-famous hotels, sandy shores and an indoor ski slope, this area is a must for any itinerary.

This stretch of coastline, between Dubai Marina and Umm Suqeim, is home to some of the most prestigious and popular resorts in Dubai. From the exclusive, iconic Burj Al Arab and Jumeirah Beach Hotel at one end, along Al Sufouh Road past the One & Only Royal Mirage, The Westin and, finally, at the other end, Le Meridien Mina Seyahi (with everyone's favourite beach party bar, Barasti (p.291), this section of the Gulf contains more pricey hotels than a Monopoly set. In the middle of all this, stretching several kilometres out to sea, is The Palm, Dubai's original mind-boggling man-made island, with its countless luxury villas and apartments, and the Disney-esque Atlantis hotel as its crowning showpiece. Within these resorts are dozens of excellent eating and drinking choices, open to all, while Souk Madinat Jumeirah (p.116) and, nearby in Al Barsha, Mall of the Emirates (p.203) are both great spots for shopping, dining and all-round entertainment.

Sun and water lovers are well catered for here too, with two waterparks (Wild Wadi and Aquaventure), a great public beach and several full-service private hotel beaches available for day use. If the beautiful weather gets to be too much, there's always Ski Dubai (p.20) where you can have a jaunt in the snow to cool you down.

## Atlantis The Palm

04 426 0000

Crescent Rd, Palm Jumeirah          www.atlantisthepalm.com

As the name suggests, the water theme is an important part of the Atlantis set-up. Aquaventure is the resort's thrilling water park; get the adrenaline pumping by making the Leap of Faith, a 27.5 metre near-vertical drop, or take the various slides that shoot you through a series of tunnels surrounded by shark-infested waters. Alternatively, The Rapids will carry you around a 2.3 kilometre river, complete with waterfalls and wave surges. Another attraction here is Dolphin Bay, where you can get close up in the water with playful bottlenose dolphins, while inside the hotel is the Lost Chambers aquarium, which contains 65,000 colourful inhabitants. The hotel is also home to several top restaurants, including Nobu (p.269) and Rostang (p.275). **Map** 1 D1 **Metro** Nakheel

## Burj Al Arab

04 301 7777

Jumeira Rd, Nr Wild Wadi, Umm Suqeim    www.jumeirah.com

The Burj Al Arab is one of the most photographed sights in Dubai. The billowing-sail structure is a stunning piece of architecture – and inside it's no less spectacular. If your budget allows, you shouldn't miss the opportunity to sample luxury at the spa, bars and restaurants. Particularly recommended is afternoon tea at Sahn Eddar (p.276) or the Skyview Bar (p.302), and fine seafood dining at Al Mahara (p.243). Keep in mind that you won't be allowed into the Burj unless you have a reservation at one of the dining venues. Advanced booking is required.

**Map** 2 D1 **Metro** Mall Of The Emirates

### Souk Madinat Jumeirah
04 366 8888

Jumeira Rd, Nr Wild Wadi, Umm Suqeim   www.jumeirah.com

Souk Madinat Jumeirah is located just a stone's throw from the Burj Al Arab and next-door neighbour of Al Qasr (p.68). Built to resemble a traditional Arabian market, the souk is a maze of alleyways featuring 75 open-fronted shops and boutiques where you can find everything from swimwear to souvenirs. For weary shoppers, there are numerous coffee shops and bars, as well as Talise (p.173), an outstanding spa. This is also a popular destination for dining, including Moroccan food at Shoo Fee Ma Fee (p.278), and Chinese fusion at Zheng He's (p.286). **Map** 2 D1 **Metro** Mall Of The Emirates

### Umm Suqeim Beach

Nr Jumeirah Beach Hotel, Umm Suqeim

This lovely stretch of sand is on the Big Bus Tour (p.139) route and is one of the busiest public beaches at the weekends, especially Fridays. Visit mid-week to enjoy the golden sands and relatively clear waters. The jetty on the right provides a good spot for snorkelling but be aware of the currents. New lifeguard centres are being constructed at intervals along the beach and, while there are no toilet facilities at present, there are several petrol stations nearby if nature calls.
**Map** 2 D1 **Metro** Mall Of The Emirates

### Wild Wadi Water Park
04 348 4444

Nr Jumeirah Beach Hotel, Umm Suqeim   www.wildwadi.com

Spread over 12 acres beside Jumeirah Beach Hotel, this water park has a host of aquatic rides and attractions to suit all ages and bravery levels. Depending on how busy it is, you may have to queue for some of the rides, but the wait is worth it. After paying the entrance fee, there is no limit to the number of times you can ride. The park opens at 10:00 and the closing time depends on the time of year. Admission is Dhs.200 for adults and Dhs.165 for children. Thursday is lady's night for those girls who'd rather not show their skin to everyone. There is also a 'sundowner' rate (for the last two hours of opening), when adults pay Dhs.165 and children below 1.1 meters pay Dhs.135.

**Map** 2 D1 **Metro** Mall Of The Emirates

If you only do one thing in...

# The Palm Jumeirah & Al Sufouh

Take in the (recreated) old by wandering Souk Madinat Jumeirah's alleyways before heading to the beach for a view of the new in the form of the Burj Al Arab.

## Best for...

**Eating & Drinking:** Sip with a view at Après (p.245) while watching people hurtle down Ski Dubai's slopes.

**Families:** Head to Atlantis' water attractions (p.115) to kick back on the lazy river, watch the dolphins or stretch out on the hotel's private beach.

**Relaxation:** Pamper yourself in the incredible luxury of Talise Spa (p.173) at Madinat Jumeirah.

**Shopping:** Mall of the Emirates is a major 'new Dubai' dining and entertainment hub – and it also has some of the region's best shopping (p.203).

**Sightseeing:** Take a ride on The Palm's monorail, which provides great views of the coastline, plus the chance to nosey at some of the island's villas (p.56).

Clockwise from top: Al Mahara, Madinat Jumeirah, Dubai's icons

# Umm Hurair: Creekside Adventure

**Once known as the leisure capital of the city, people now flock to this area for luxury shopping, lazy afternoons and family fun.**

Together, Oud Metha, Umm Hurair and Zabeel form a park-filled corner of Dubai that lines the bottom half of the creek. Wafi (p.209) in Umm Hurair and Lamcy Plaza in Oud Metha are popular shopping spots for both bargains and international fashion labels. The addition of Raffles Dubai (p.69) to the Wafi complex has improved the area's already impressive restaurant and bar roster. This is also the home of Healthcare City and the Grand Hyatt, which hosts several top restaurants. You'll find some of the city's best family leisure options here too, including Creekside Park and the amazing new children's centre, Stargate.

### Children's City

04 334 0808

Creekside Park, Gate 1, Umm Hurair  www.childrencity.ae

Children's City offers kids hands-on, educational amusement facilities. There's a planetarium, a nature centre, and the Discovery Space, revealing the miracles of the human body. It is aimed at 5 to 12 year olds, although toddlers and teenagers might find it entertaining. The centre opens daily from 09:00 to 20:00, except on Fridays when it opens at 15:00. Entrance costs Dhs.10 for children under 16 and Dhs.15 for anyone over 16. **Map** 5 B7 **Metro** Healthcare City

## Creekside Park

Nr Wonderland Theme & Water Park, Umm Hurair

Creekside Park is blessed with acres of gardens, fishing piers, barbecue sites, children's play areas, restaurants and kiosks. Running along the park's 2.5km stretch of creek frontage is a cable car system, allowing visitors an unrestricted view from 30m in the air. You'll find Children's City here (p.120), and from Gate Two, four-wheel cycles can be hired for Dhs.20 per hour. Admission costs Dhs.5. **Map** 5 B7 **Metro** Oud Metha

## Stargate

800 9977

Zabeel Park, Area A, Gate 4, Zabeel    www.stargatedubai.com

Kids will love Stargate; this massive complex, located in Zabeel Park, is free to enter, with access to the five giant play domes paid for by a rechargeable card. Each area contains a different adventure; there's a multi-storey soft-play area, two go-kart tracks, an ice rink, an indoor rollercoaster and a 3D fun zone. The walkways connecting the play domes house plenty of food venues, retail outlets, and arcade games. **Map** 1 P4 **Metro** Al Jafiliya

## Zabeel Park

Nr Trade Centre R/A, Zabeel

Providing an oasis of greenery in dusty Dubai, Zabeel Park has several recreational areas, a jogging track, a mini cricket pitch, a football field, boating lake and an amphitheatre, plus a number of restaurants and cafes. Mondays are ladies only. Entry costs Dhs.5 for anyone over 2 years old. **Map** 1 P4 **Metro** Al Jafiliya

**Exploring**

**Umm Hurair: Creekside Adventure**

MAKE UP FOR EVER

## If you only do one thing in...
# Umm Hurair

Sample the joys of shopping, spas and oversized cocktails all under one roof at Wafi (p.209).

## Best for...

**Eating & Drinking:** There are plenty of top restaurants at Wafi, but the modern Indian cuisine of Asha's (p.246) truly captures the imagination.

**Families:** Let the children loose at Stargate (p.121) – great fun for adults too.

**Relaxation:** Take a picnic to Creekside Park (p.121) and watch the park and creek action unfold.

**Shopping:** Find unforgettable gifts at the underground souk of Khan Murjan (p.192).

**Sightseeing:** Squeeze into a cable car in Creekside Park (p.121) for great views over the water.

Clockwise from top: Raffles, Wafi, Creekside Park

# Off The Beaten Track

**Some of Dubai's best-kept cultural secrets are found in some of the most unlikely places.**

Outside of the areas already covered in this chapter, there are some sightseeing highlights dotted around other parts of town. The area of Karama is famous for its markets that hawk counterfeit goods and restaurants serving cheap south-Asian dinners, Satwa is home to some of the best people watching in the city, and the dusty industrial park, Al Quoz, hosts several of the most cutting-edge art galleries in the region.

## Gallery Isabelle Van Den Eynde
04 323 5052

17 Al Serkal Ave, 8th St, Al Quoz 1 www.ivde.net

This progressive art gallery represents around 20 Middle Eastern artists and is partnered with galleries in Europe. The result is a destination where collectors can source artwork and get advice on everything from finance to framing. Even if you're not in the market to buy, Gallery Isabelle van den Eynde hosts exhibitions by its steadily growing roster of talent. Open 10:00 to 19:00 Saturday to Thursday.
**Map** 1 H4 **Metro** Noor Islamic Bank

## Global Village
04 362 4114

Emirates Rd, Dubailand www.globalvillage.ae

Between the end of November and February, a huge plot of paved desert outside of Dubai blossoms into a celebration of multiculturalism and fairground fun. There are plenty of big rides and action-oriented shows to entertain the family, but the main attraction is the shopping. Vendors come from over 45 countries in Africa, Asia and the Middle East to showcase their cultural wares. Much of the clothing, furniture and decorations on sale are less-than-attractive, but each area has shops full of gifts and knick-knacks you can't find anywhere else in Dubai. **Map** 1 G10 **Metro** Mall Of The Emirates

## Iranian Mosque

Al Wasl Road, Jumeira

Non-Muslims can't enter the Iranian Mosque, but it's still worth admiring (and photographing) from the outside. The blue mosaic tiling, pillars, arches and elaborate minarets are typical of Persian architecture, making this one of the most photogenic sights in Dubai. The mosque also serves as a stunning counterpoint to some of the modern places of worship you'll see elsewhere in the city.
**Map** 1 N3 **Metro** Trade Centre

## The Jam Jar

04 341 7303

Nr Dubai Garden Ctr, Al Quoz          www.thejamjardubai.com

The Jam Jar is injecting a little culture to Sheikh Zayed Road. This small, bright gallery also offers wannabe Picassos the chance to paint for a fixed price that includes unlimited paint, brushes and soft drinks. Prices start at Dhs.35 and rise to Dhs.195, depending on canvas size. Open 10:00 to 20:00 Monday to Thursday and Saturday, 14:00 to 20:00 on Friday and closed Sunday. **Map** 1 G4 **Metro** First Gulf Bank

## Karama

Primarily a residential area consisting of relatively low-cost flats in low-rise apartment blocks, Karama is well known for having something for everyone. It has a great shopping area, which is particularly notorious for its imitation goods, and the popular Karama Shopping Complex (p.191). Karama's merchants are a far cry from their mall counterparts and offer a challenge if you like practising your haggling skills. There's a great range of inexpensive restaurants serving tasty Indian and Pakistani cuisine, including Saravana Bhavan (p.276) and Karachi Darbar (04 334 7272).
**Map** 5 A4 **Metro** Al Karama

## Opera Gallery                                          04 323 0909

Dubai International Financial
  Centre (DIFC), Trade Centre          www.operagallery.com
Part of an international chain, Opera Gallery opened in 2008 in Dubai International Financial Centre. It has a permanent collection of art on display and for sale, mainly European and Chinese, with visiting exhibitions changing throughout the year. The permanent collection also includes several masterpieces, so look out for the odd Dali or Picasso.
**Map** 2 G5 **Metro** Financial Centre

## Plant Street

Nr Satwa Rd & Al Wasl Rd, Satwa
Famous for pots and plants, pet shops, fabric shops and hardware outlets, Plant Street is another spot that hasn't changed much since the beginning of Dubai's boom. Head

Global Village

here on a Saturday evening to soak up the atmosphere, but women are advised to cover up to avoid being stared at. **Map** 1 N3 **Metro** Trade Centre

## The Third Line

04 341 1367

Nr Times Square, Al Quoz                              www.thethirdline.com

One of the leading lights of the Dubai art scene, The Third Line gallery in Al Quoz hosts exhibitions by artists originating from or working in the Middle East. There are indoor and outdoor spaces for shows, many of which have caught the eye of both local and international collectors. The gallery is open Saturday to Thursday 10:00 to 19: 00; it is closed on Fridays. **Map** 1 H5 **Metro** Noor Islamic Bank

# Further Out

**The United Arab Emirates offers visitors some spectacular sights, from modern cities to ancient forts, and mountain pools to seemingly infinite deserts.**

If you are on holiday in Dubai for longer than a few days, you should definitely build time into your schedule to explore the rest of the country. Hire a car or book a tour and hit the road. This part of the world has a lot to offer, and many of the sights are just a short drive away. Close to Dubai, nature lovers should check out Ras Al Khor Wildlife Sanctuary (Ras Al Khor Road, 04 606 6822), the only nature reserve within the city and a great place for bird watchers, with 1,500 flamingos, while once outside the urban sprawl you'll quickly be surrounded by rolling sand dunes, wandering camels and imposing mountains. Quite simply, heading out of Dubai to the other cities and emirates can be hugely rewarding and will add a worthy cultural perspective to your time in the UAE.

## Abu Dhabi

Dubai is often mistaken as the capital of the UAE – but that honour actually belongs to Abu Dhabi. Oil was discovered there before Dubai (1958 compared with 1966) and today it accounts for 10% of the world's known crude oil reserves, making it the richest emirate. It is home to numerous internationally renowned hotels, a selection of shiny shopping malls and a sprinkling of culture in the form of heritage sites and souks. The malls are much less busy than in Dubai, and goods are sometimes cheaper.

Travellers to the city shouldn't miss the Sheikh Zayed Grand Mosque (800555, www.visitabudhabi.ae). The recently finished mosque covers 22,000 sqm and is the sixth-largest in the world. During the cooler months, the blue tile-covered corniche on the gulf-side of the city is a great place for an evening stroll. Abu Dhabi has big plans to build up its international appeal as a tourist destination; Formula 1 took place in the country for the first time in 2009, and both the Louvre and Guggenheim museums are being brought to town in the near future.

Outside the city, Abu Dhabi emirate is home to the oasis towns of Al Ain and Liwa. Al Ain is Abu Dhabi's second city and certainly worthy of a visit (see p.129). South-west of Abu Dhabi is the Liwa oasis, where the spectacular dunes are a photographer's dream. Liwa lies at the edge of the Rub Al Khali (Empty Quarter), one of the largest sand deserts in the world.

## Al Ain

Al Ain is a city of great historic significance in the UAE thanks to its strategic location on ancient trading routes between Oman and the Gulf, and because of its fertile oases. The birthplace of the late, revered Sheikh Zayed, Al Ain is known as the Garden City, and is filled with several date plantations and pockets of greenery. These oases (there are seven in total) are lovely places to explore; drive around the networks of walled, cobbled roads, park up, and wander through the lush green plantations, complete with working falaj irrigation systems. You might even get to taste some fresh fruit if you stumble across some harvested bounty (be sure to ask permission from the picker before you pop one in your mouth though). Next to the main Al Ain Oasis is the interesting Al Ain Museum (03 764 1595, www.aam.gov. ae), which illustrates various aspects of life in the UAE and includes a selection of photographs, Bedouin jewellery and archeological displays. One of the city's best attractions is the revamped Al Ain Wildlife Park & Resort (03 782 8188, www. awpr.ae), at the foot of Jebel Hafeet. Conservation is the keyword here, with natural habitats recreated to be as near to the real thing as possible, and you can get the whole family up close to animals including giraffes, zebras and rhinos.

For a great view over the city and expansive desert landscape, take a drive up Jebel Hafeet. The winding road rises right to the summit, where you'll find the Mercure Grand Jebel Hafeet hotel – a great place for an overnight stay or just a refreshing drink with a terrific view (03 783 8888, www.mercure.com).

## East Coast

Even if you're only in the UAE for a short time, a trip to the East Coast is a must. You can get there in less than two hours.

The diving is considered better than that off Dubai's coast, mainly because of increased visibility. Snoopy Island off Dibba's coast is a favourite spot for snorkelling. The East Coast is home to a few interesting spots, many of which are free to explore. The site of the oldest mosque in the UAE, Bidiyah, is roughly half way down the East Coast, north of Khor Fakkan. The building is believed to date back to the middle of the 15th century and was restored in 2003. The village is considered one of the oldest settlements on the East Coast, which is thought to have been inhabited since 3000BC. Located at the northernmost point of the East Coast, Dibba is made up of three fishing villages, each coming under a different jurisdiction: Sharjah, Fujairah, and Oman. The villages share an attractive bay and excellent diving locations. The Hajar Mountains provide a wonderful backdrop to the public beaches. Further north across the border into Oman is Khasab, a great base for exploring the inlets and unspoilt waters of Musandam. You can stay at the Golden Tulip (+968 26 73 07 77; www.goldentulipkhasab.com), which can organise dhow cruises and dolphin watching, both of which are recommended, or the luxurious Six Senses Hideaway Zighy Bay (+968 26 735 555; www.sixsenses.com).

Further south on the coast lies Fujairah, the youngest of the seven emirates. Overlooking the atmospheric old town is a fort that is reportedly about 300 years old. The surrounding hillsides are dotted with more such ancient forts and watchtowers, which add an air of mystery and charm. Dubai residents often use Fujairah as a base for exploring the rest of the coast. Hotels include Le Meridien Al Aqah (09 244 9000; www.lemeridien-alaqah.com), and JAL Fujairah Hotel & Spa (09 244 9700; www.jalfujairahresort.ae).

Khor Kalba sits just south of Fujairah and is the most northerly mangrove forest in the world, and home to a variety of plant, marine and birdlife not found anywhere else in the UAE. A canoe tour by Desert Rangers (p.139) is the best way to reach the heart of the mangrove reserve.

# Hatta

The road leading to Hatta from Dubai (E44) is a trip in itself. Watch as the sand gradually changes from beige to dark orange and then disappears, only to be replaced by jagged mountains. The famous Big Red sand dune lies on this road, and is a popular spot for dune driving in 4WDs or quad bikes.

Hatta is a small town, nestled at the food of the Hajar Mountains, about 100km from Dubai city and 10km from the Dubai-Oman border. It is home to the oldest fort in Dubai emirate, which was built in 1790. You'll also see several watchtowers on the surrounding hills. On the drive you'll pass a row of carpet shops, ideal for putting your bargaining skills into practise. The town itself has a sleepy, relaxed feel, and includes the Heritage Village (04 852 1374), which charts the area's 3,000 year history and includes a 200 year-old mosque and the fortress built by Sheikh Maktoum bin Hasher Al Maktoum in 1896, which is now used as a weaponry museum.

The Hatta Fort Hotel (04 852 3211, www.jebelali-international.com) offers bungalow-style luxury rooms and plenty of sports and leisure facilities including shooting and mini-golf.

Beyond the village and into the mountains are the Hatta Pools, where you can see deep, strangely shaped canyons carved out by rushing floodwater. For tours see p.138.

The trail towards the pools is graded, so a two-wheel drive car and some skilled driving should be enough to get you there. To get to the pools from the Dubai-Hatta road, take a right at the fort roundabout, then left towards the Heritage Village, another left at the roundabout, and then the first

# explorer tours
### an expression of passion

## explore with us.
**Nobody knows the Arabian Peninsula like Explorer Tours**

## EXPLORER TOURS
P.O. Box: 76654, Dubai, U.A.E.
Tel: +971 4 2861991 Fax: +971 4 2861994
E-mail: info@explorertours.ae Visit: www.explorertours.ae

main right. After driving through a second village, the tarmac will end and you will see a gravel track on your right.

# Northern Emirates

North of Dubai and Sharjah are Ajman, Umm Al Quwain and Ras Al Khaimah. These three emirates are much smaller in size than Dubai and Abu Dhabi and are also less developed.

Ajman is the smallest of the emirates, but its proximity to Dubai and Sharjah has enabled it to grow considerably. It was once known as one of the largest dhow building centres in the region, and while it is mainly modern boats that emerge from the yards these days, you can still catch a glimpse of a traditionally built dhow sailing out to sea. Ajman also has some great beaches and a pleasant corniche. Much of the nightlife revolves around the Ajman Kempinski Hotel & Resort (06 714 5555, www.kempinski.com/ajman).

Umm Al Quwain has the smallest population and little has changed over the years. It is home to the expansive Dreamland Aqua Park (www.dreamlanduae.com). Two of the most interesting activities Umm Al Quwain has to offer are crab hunting and mangrove tours. The Flamingo Beach Resort (06 765 0000, www.flamingoresort.ae) offers both tours.

Ras Al Khaimah is the most northerly of the seven emirates but you can make the trip from Dubai in around an hour on the Emirates Road. With the jagged Hajar Mountains rising just behind the city, and the Arabian Gulf stretching out from the shore, RAK has some of the best scenery in the UAE. A creek divides the city into the old town and the newer Al Nakheel district. For a day trip, you should go the souk in the old town and the National Museum of Ras Al Khaimah (07 233 3411, www.rakmuseum.gov.ae). This is a good starting point for exploring the surrounding countryside and visiting the ancient sites of Ghalilah and Shimal.

# Sharjah

Before Dubai's rise to prominence as a trading and tourism hotspot, neighbouring Sharjah was one of the wealthiest towns in the region, with settlers earning their livelihood from fishing, pearling and trade. Sharjah is worth a visit for its various museums and great shopping. Its commitment to art, culture and preserving its traditional heritage is well known throughout the Arab world. Sharjah is built around Khalid Lagoon (popularly known as the creek), and the surrounding Buheirah Corniche is a popular spot for an evening stroll. From various points on the lagoon, small dhows can be hired to see the lights of the city from the water.

The Heritage Area (06 569 3999, www.sharjahtourism.ae) is a fascinating old walled city, home to numerous museums and the traditional Souk Al Arsah. The nearby Arts Area is a treat for art lovers with galleries and more museums. A must is Al Qasba (06 556 0777, www.qaq.ae), Sharjah's latest attraction which has performance spaces and waterside restaurants. Another worthy stop-off is the Sharjah Natural History & Botanical Museum (06 531 1411, www.sharjahmuseums.ae).

Shoppers shouldn't miss the beautiful Central Souk, also known as the Blue Souk. The two buildings contain more than 600 shops selling gold and knick-knacks. This is one of the best places in the UAE to buy carpets.

# Oman

Just a few hours from Dubai, you'll find the countless attractions of Oman. It's a peaceful and breathtaking country, with history, culture and spectacular scenery. The capital, Muscat, has enough attractions to keep you busy for a short break, including beautiful beaches, some great restaurants and cafes, and the mesmerising old souk at Mutrah. Out of the capital, you will find many historic old towns and forts, and some of the most stunning mountain and wadi scenery in the region. Salalah in the south has the added bonus of being cool and wet in the summer. Isolated from the rest of the country, on the tip of the Arabian Peninsula, is the Omani enclave of Musandam. With its jagged mountains and fjord-like inlets, it has the moniker 'the Norway of the Middle East' and is a must-visit if you are in Dubai for any serious length of time.

Ras Al Jinz is a small fishing village on the Ras Al Hadd Turtle Reserve. The protected beach is where endangered green turtles come to nest and visitors can see the huge turtles by booking a guided tour with Ras Al Jinz Scinetific & Visitor Centre (+968 965 50606/0707, www.rasaljinz-turtlereserve. com) which has a small guesthouse, restaurant and a gift shop.

A flight from Dubai to Muscat takes 45 minutes, but when you factor in check-in times and customs it's not much quicker than driving. There are daily flights from Dubai with Emirates and Oman Air, while Air Arabia flies from Sharjah. Regular flights to Salalah from Dubai are also available. It is possible to drive to Musandam from Dubai in around three hours, but make sure your hire car insurance covers Oman. For further information see the *Oman Mini Visitors' Guide*.

# Ras Al Jinz Scientific & Visitors Centre

- Guided evening and morning Turtle Nesting tours
- Tented luxury accommodation – to start by Feb 2011
- Restaurant serving breakfast, lunch and Dinner
- 12 Well appointed Guest rooms
- Turtle Gallery (Museum) – to start by Feb 2011
- Souvenir shop

Oman's world class nature conservation beach for 'Green Turtles' managed by responsible children of Mother nature!

المركز العلمي لخدمات الزوار ومحمية السلاحف برأس الجنز
**Ras Al Jinz Scientific & Visitor Centre**
Sur, Sultanate of Oman

Phone: +968 96550606/0707
Fax.: +968 95300234
Email: reservations@rasaljinz-turtlereserve.com
www.rasaljinz-turtlereserve.com

# Tours & Sightseeing

**Whether it be by plane, boat or 4WD, taking a tour is a fun and efficient way to see a different side of the Emirates.**

Navigating the city by taxi or Metro can be pretty easy, but exploring the surrounding areas often proves a bit more difficult without the help of a guide. Boat tours are a great way to see the city from afar while enjoying the clear Gulf waters; helicopter and plane tours give the most extensive look at the growing city; and bus tours offer plenty of information and more user-friendly schedules.

No visitor should leave without experiencing a desert safari of some sort. Expert drivers blast 4WDs up, down and around massive dunes while passing old Bedouin villages and pointing out incredible natural attractions. Mountain safaris lead passengers through the narrow wadis of the Hajar Mountains. Most driving safaris include pickup from your hotel and lunch. Some end the day of driving at a replica Bedouin camp where passengers can watch a belly dancer, eat Arabic delicacies and smoke shisha. Some operators run overnight safaris that combine half-day treks with a driving adventure.

While most of the companies listed below offer a wide range of experiences, some are more specialised. Both Aerogulf Services and Seawings concentrate on plane tours, Balloon Adventures is the city's main balloon ride operator, The Big Bus Company is the premier bus tour provider, and Bristol Middle East concentrates on boat and yacht tours.

## Tours & Sightseeing

| | | |
|---|---|---|
| **Absolute Adventure** | 04 345 9900 | www.adventure.ae |
| **Aerogulf Services Company** | 04 220 0331 | www.aerogulfservices.com |
| **Alpha Tours** | 04 294 9888 | www.alphatoursdubai.com |
| **Arabian Adventures** | 04 303 4888 | www.arabian-adventures.com |
| **Balloon Adventures Emirates** | 04 285 4949 | www.ballooning.ae |
| **Bristol Middle East Yacht Solution** | 04 366 3538 | www.bristol-middleeast.com |
| **Desert Adventures Tourism** | 04 224 2800 | www.desertadventures.com |
| **Desert Rangers** | 04 357 2233 | www.desertrangers.com |
| **Dubai Tourist & Travel Services** | 04 336 7727 | www.dubai-travel.ae |
| **Gulf Ventures** | 04 404 5880 | www.gulfventures.ae |
| **Knight Tours** | 04 343 7725 | www.knighttours.ae |
| **Net Tours** | 04 266 6655 | www.nettoursdubai.com |
| **Oasis Palm Tourism** | 04 262 8889 | www.opdubai.com |
| **Off-Road Adventures** | 050 628 9667 | www.arabiantours.com |
| **Orient Tours** | 04 282 8238 | www.orienttours.ae |
| **Seawings** | 807 0708 | www.seawings.ae |
| **The Big Bus Company** | 04 340 7709 | www.bigbustours.com |
| **Tour Dubai** | 04 336 8409 | www.tour-dubai.com |
| **Travco** | 04 336 6643 | www.travcotravel.com |
| **Safe Way Tourism** | 04 345 4504 | |
| **Wonder Bus Tours** | 04 359 5656 | www.wonderbustours.net |

# Sports & Spas

# Active Dubai

**Dubai has a wealth of spas, sports and resorts dedicated to the art of relaxation.**

It is not just shops and beaches that attract visitors to Dubai. Numerous world-class sporting events take place in the city throughout the year, drawing crowds of residents and tourists alike. The Dubai World Cup is the richest horse race in the world, the Dubai Rugby Sevens regularly pulls in crowds in excess of 70,000 and the Dubai Tennis Championships see the world's leading players compete in an intimate setting.

Dubai is also home to several excellent golf courses, many designed by leading figures such as Robert Trent Jones II, Colin Montgomerie and Nick Faldo.

Traditional Arabian sports, such as camel racing and falconry, offer an interesting perspective on local heritage, and should not be missed.

A combination of Arabian Gulf shoreline and the vast expanses of desert just outside the city make Dubai a great adventure sports destination: from kitesurfing and diving to dune driving and sand skiing, there are many opportunities for unique and exciting sports activities.

All this activity aside, those who are seeking blissful holidays spent relaxing and rejuvenating will find a collection of world-class spas offering a range of unique treatments in luxurious surroundings, usually at surprisingly reasonable prices.

Clockwise from top left: climbing Fossil Rock, underwater life, Dubai Tennis Championships

# Sports & Activities

Miles of sand dunes, clear seas, classic Arabian heritage and superb sports facilities: holidays in Dubai are packed with unique sporting opportunities.

## Dhow Charters

### Al Boom Tourist Village

04 324 3000

Nr Al Garhoud Bridge, Umm Hurair · www.alboom.ae

Al Boom Tourist Village operates nine dhows on the creek, ranging from single-deckers with room for 20 people, right up to the huge triple-decker Mumtaz, which can take 350 passengers. It offers a variety of packages, with prices varying accordingly. As well as the usual dinner cruises, late-night trips can also be arranged. **Map** 5 B8 **Metro** Healthcare City

### Khasab Travel & Tours

04 266 9950

Warba Centre, Deira · www.khasabtours.com

Sailing north from Dibba, this cruise follows the coastline where steep rocky cliffs rise out of the sea. You'll pass small fishing villages and will hopefully see dolphins and turtles. Prices start at Dhs.200 per adult for a full day, including lunch and refreshments. **Map** 1 R4 **Metro** Abu Baker Al Siddique

## Golf

The number of international-standard courses grows each year, with recent additions including the Al Badia Golf Club

InterContinental Dubai Festival City (p.146). Plans for the world's first course designed by Tiger Woods is in development in Dubailand and was set to open in late 2009, but construction is still very much in progress. The Els Club, designed by South Africa's 'Big Easy' Ernie Els, is within the same development.

Dubai Golf operates a central reservation system for the major courses in the emirate. For further information visit www.dubaigolf.com or email booking@dubaigolf.com.

### Arabian Ranches Golf Club                04 366 3000

Emirates Rd,
Arabian Ranches                www.arabianranchesgolfdubai.com

Designed by Ian Baker-Finch in association with Nicklaus Design, this par 72 grass course uses the natural desert terrain and features indigenous shrubs and bushes. You must have an official handicap to play, but can reserve a tee-off time six days in advance. Facilities include a golf academy with floodlit driving range, an extensive short game practice area, and GPS on all golf carts.  Map 1 E9

### Dubai Creek Golf & Yacht Club                04 295 6000

Baniyas Rd, Nr Deira City Centre                www.dubaigolf.com

This par 71 championship course is open to all players holding a valid handicap certificate. The challenging front nine was designed by Thomas Björn; there is also a nine-hole par three course, a floodlit driving range and extensive short game practice facilities. Those who are new to the game are encouraged to join the golf academy manned by PGA-qualified instructors.  Map 5 C8  Metro GGICO

### The Els Club Dubai
04 425 1010

Emirates Rd, Dubai Sports City    www.elsclubdubai.com

Ernie Els designed this 18 hole signature course, which has become extremely popular with Dubai's golfers – the first batch of memberships sold out within hours. The club features the Butch Harmon School of Golf, and a stadium that has the capacity to seat 60,000. A massive Mediterranean clubhouse is still under construction and will be managed by internationally renowned Troon Golf. **Map** 1 C8

### Emirates Golf Club
04 380 2222

Shk Zayed Rd, Int 5, Emirates Living    www.dubaigolf.com

Emirates Golf Club has two 18 hole championship courses – the par 71 Majlis Course was the first grass course in the Middle East and it hosts the annual Dubai Desert Classic (p.157), and the Wadi Course. The club also offers the Peter Cowen Golf Academy, along with two driving ranges and dedicated practice areas. **Map** 2 B2 **Metro** Nakheel

### Al Badia Golf Club
04 601 0101

Al Rebat St, Festival City    www.albadiagolfclub.ae

World-renowned golf course designer Robert Trent Jones II is behind the InterContinental's offering. Lying at the heart of Dubai Festival City, beside the creek, the resort enjoys great views across the city. The 7,303 yard par 72 Championship Course has a plush clubhouse and extensive water features. **Map** 1 Q7 **Metro** Emirates

Golf in Dubai

## Jebel Ali Golf Resort & Spa
04 814 5555
Nr Palm Jebel Ali, Jebel Ali    www.jebelali-international.com

Situated in the landscaped gardens of the Jebel Ali Golf Resort & Spa, this nine-hole, par 36 course offers views of the Arabian Gulf. Renowned for its good condition all year, the course is also home to the Jebel Ali Golf Resort & Spa Challenge, the opener for the Dubai Desert Classic (p.157). **Map** 1 A4

## Montgomerie Golf Club
04 390 5600
The Address Montgomerie Dubai, Emirates Living    www.themontgomerie.com

Designed by Colin Montgomerie and Desmond Muirhead, the 18 hole, par 72 course has some unique characteristics, including the 656 yard 18th hole. Golfing facilities include a driving range, a floodlit par three course and a swing analysis studio, while the clubhouse boasts guest rooms, a spa, bars and restaurants such as Nineteen (p.269).
**Map** 2 A3  **Metro** Nakheel

# Hot Air Ballooning & Parasailing

Balloon Adventures Emirates (04 285 4949), Amigos Balloons (04 289 9295, www.amigos-balloons.com) and Desert Rangers (04 357 2233) offer trips across the desert in a hot air balloon. Journeys with Amigos Balloons cost Dhs.950 per person and set off from a variety of locations – you can also go for a private flight for two for Dhs.3,500. If you'd like an aerial view of the Palm Jumeirah but can't afford a balloon then try parasailing. The Sheraton Jumeirah Beach Resort (04 399 5533) has a watersports and an activity centre, and Nautica 1992 (050 426 2415) operates from the Habtoor Grand. Summertime Marine Sports (04 257 3084) also offers flights from the open beach near Le Meridien Mina Seyahi hotel (04 399 3333). All use specially designed boats with winches and a launch pad on the back, so you don't have to sprint down the beach to get airborne. You can expect to pay around Dhs.250 for a 15 to 20 minute ride or Dhs.350 for the tandem option – however, prices vary depending on the length of and option of the ride.

# Wadi & Dune Bashing

Most car rental agencies offer visitors 4WDs capable of desert driving. If renting a 4WD, make sure you get the details of the insurance plan, as many rental insurers won't cover damage caused by off-roading. Dune bashing, or desert driving, is one of the toughest challenges for both car and driver, but once you have mastered it, it's a lot of fun.

If you do venture out into the desert, it is a good idea to have at least one experienced driver and one other car to

Come fly with me!

www.amigos-balloons.com

# AMIGOS BALLOONS

Tel: + 971 4 28 99 295

Email: fly@amigos-balloons.com

Mobile: + 971 50 73 562 37

www.amigos-balloons.com

help tow you out if you get stuck. Most major tour companies offer a range of desert and mountain safaris if you'd rather leave the driving to the professionals.

Driving in wadis is usually a bit more straightforward. Wadis are (usually) dry gullies, carved through the rock by rushing floodwaters, following the course of seasonal rivers. The main safety precaution to take when wadi bashing is to keep your eyes open for rare, but not impossible, thunder storms developing. The wadis can fill up quickly and you will need to make your way to higher ground pretty fast to avoid flash floods. For further information and tips on off-road driving in the UAE, check out the *UAE Off-Road Explorer*.

## Watersports & Diving

Most beachside hotels offer both guests and visitors a range of watersports, including sea kayaking, sailing and windsurfing. Some hotels require that non-guests pay beach fees in order to access the facilities, while others will let you enter the beach area for free if you make a reservation at the watersports desk beforehand. Contact the Habtoor Grand Resort (04 399 5000) and Le Meridien Mina Seyahi (04 399 3333).

Diving is popular and the clear waters off the coast are home to a variety of marine species, coral life and even shipwrecks. You'll see some exotic fish and possibly moray eels, small sharks, barracuda, sea snakes and stingrays. Most of the wrecks are on the west coast, while the flora and fauna can be seen on the east coast. Another option for diving enthusiasts is a trip to Musandam. Part of the Sultanate of Oman (p.136), it is often described as the 'Norway of the

Middle East' due to its many inlets and cliffs that plunge directly into the sea.

Sheer wall dives with strong currents and clear waters are more suitable for advanced divers, while the huge bays with their calm waters and bountiful shallow reefs are ideal for the less experienced. Courses are offered under the usual international training organisations. More details on specific dives and sites can be found in the *UAE Underwater Explorer*.

## Al Boom Diving
04 342 2993

Al Wasl Rd, Villa 254, Nr Iranian
Hospital, Jumeira
www.alboomdiving.com

Al Boom Diving is a purpose-built school with a fully outfitted diving shop. A variety of courses are held both here and at its PADI Gold Palm Resort at Le Meridien Al Aqah Beach Resort (09 244 9000) near Fujairah. It also offers the chance to dive with the sharks in The Dubai Mall aquarium (p.200).
**Map** 1 N3 **Metro** Emirates Towers

## The Pavilion Dive Centre
04 406 8827

Jumeirah Beach Hotel,
Umm Suqeim
www.thepaviliondivecentre.com

This centre is run by PADI course directors, who offer courses for beginners through to instructors. Daily dive charters for certified divers are available in Dubai, and trips to Musandam can be organised upon request. Two dives with full equipment are priced at Dhs.300 in Dubai or Dhs.490 in Musandam (including transport and lunch).
**Map** 2 D1 **Metro** Mall of the Emirates

### Scuba Dubai

04 341 4940

Al Khail Rd, Al Quoz · www.scubadubai.com

For those wishing to arrange their own diving and snorkelling trips, equipment can be rented from Scuba Dubai on a 24 hour basis. Rates for Thursday, Friday and Saturday are the same as renting for one day because the shop is closed on Fridays. Note that original diving certification must be shown for all equipment rentals. **Map** 3 D1 **Metro** First Gulf Bank

### Scubatec

04 334 8988

Sana Building, Al Karama

Scubatec is a five-star IDC, licensed by PADI and TDI. Lessons are provided in Arabic, English, German or Urdu, and the company offers a full range of courses from beginner to instructor level. A variety of dive trips is available in Dubai and on the East Coast. **Map** 5 A4 **Metro** Al Karama

## Skiing & Snowboarding

When temperatures outside are melting your sunglasses, you can go sub-zero with a visit to Ski Dubai (04 409 4000, www. skidxb.com). The huge tube extending behind and above the Mall of the Emirates (p.203) is home to five slopes to suit all skill levels, from gentle beginner slopes to the world's first indoor 'black' run. There's also a 90m long quarter pipe and the largest indoor snow park in the world. The slope has both chair lifts and tow lifts, and there's a well-stocked retail shop selling skis, boards, and clothing. Strict rules ensure only suitably skilled skiers and boarders can take to the slopes, but lessons are also offered with qualified instructors. Entrance to

the Snow Park is Dhs.120 for adults and Dhs.110 for children. Prices for a two-hour Ski Slope Pass start at Dhs.180 for adults and Dhs.150 for kids, which include all equipment and clothing (except gloves).

## Motorsports

The UAE deserts provide ideal locations for rallying, and many events are organised throughout the year by the Emirates Motor Sports Federation (EMSF). The highest profile event is the Abu Dhabi Desert Challenge (www.uaedesertchallenge.com), which is one of the top events in World Cup Cross Country Rallying. Other events throughout the year include the Spring Desert Rally (4WD), Peace Rally (saloons), Jeep Jamboree (safari), Drakkar Noir 1000 Dunes Rally (4WD), Shell Festival Parade, Audi Driving Skills (driving challenge) and Federation Rally (4WD). For details, call EMSF (04 282 7111) or visit the website (www.emsfuae.com). Yas Island (02 696 4444, www.yasisland. ae) is a new development in Abu Dhabi that will feature various attractions and amenities. The Yas Island Marina Circuit is part of the development and its 5.55km racetrack and covered grandstand seating area for 50,000 spectators is the venue for the 2010 season finale of the Formula 1 Etihad Airways Grand Prix in November (www.yasmarinacircuit.com).

## Simulated Fun

Dubai's malls have fantastic entertainment; try sky diving at Playnation, Mirdif City Centre (p.206) or for the biggest selection, head to SEGA Republic at The Dubai Mall (p.200) which has motor racing, a jungle safari and a bobsleigh simulator for big (and little) kids to try.

Ski Dubai

### Dubai Autodrome
04 367 8700

Nr Arabian Ranches, Dubailand    www.dubaiautodrome.com

The Dubai Autodrome (part of Dubailand, on Emirates Road) is the home of motorsport in Dubai. It has six different track configurations, including a 5.39km FIA-sanctioned GP circuit, premium pit facilities and a 7,000 seat grandstand. The venue hosts events throughout the year, including rounds of the FIA GT Championships. You can experience the thrill of driving on a racetrack with the guidance of qualified instructors. A range of packages and experiences is offered, including a track taster session in Audi TTs with prices starting from Dhs.750. Wannabe Alonsos of any age can burn rubber at the kartdrome. After a safety briefing, you'll take to your powerful 390cc kart (there are smaller 120cc karts for the kids) and hit the tarmac on the exciting 1.2km circuit. **Map** 1 E8

# Spectator Sports

Dubai has the best line-up of international sport in the region, with world-class tennis, golf and horse racing among the highlights.

A good range of sporting events is organised in Dubai and the emirate is steadily backing more big international events that not only capture the local imagination, but also draw sporting enthusiasts from around the world. A big advantage is that crowds are smaller and tickets for larger events are more freely available than they would be in other countries, though you'll have to be quick. Horseracing, desert rallies and motorsports are very popular as are local sports like camel racing.

## Camel Racing

This is a chance to see a truly traditional local sport. Races take place in the winter months and additional games are often held on public holidays. Races were previously held at the track at Nad Al Sheba, but this has closed to make way for Meydan

### Camel Rides

Take a short camel ride along the beach near the Hilton Dubai Jumeirah or as part of a desert safari – it's a great way to experience this traditional mode of transport. The lumbering clumsiness of the camel standing up when you first hop on forms a marked contrast to the surprising smoothness of the ride itself.

City. To find the new location, head up the Al Ain Road, past the Dubai Outlet Mall, until you reach the Al Lisali exit. Turn right off this exit and you will see the track on your right. Races are usually held early on a Friday morning, but you should see camels being exercised during the day in the cooler months.

## Golf

### Dubai Desert Classic
04 380 2112

Emirates Golf Club,
Emirates Living          www.dubaidesertclassic.com

One of the highlights of the Dubai sporting calendar, this European PGA Tour competition is a popular event among both players and spectators at the end of January and start of February. Top golfers who have previously competed in the event include Tiger Woods, Ernie Elis and Henrik Stenson.
**Map** 2 B2 **Metro** Nakheel

### Dubai World Championship
04 375 2222

Jumeirah Golf Estates    www.dubaiworldchampionship.com

The Dubai World Championship is the grand finale of The Race to Dubai, the European Tour's season-long competition which features 50 tournaments in 27 destinations. This annual tournament runs for four days and is open to the leading 60 players in The Race to Dubai rankings after the 49th event, ensuring that the cream of the golf world qualifies for the chance to compete for a prize fund of $7.5 million, with an additional $7.5 million bonus pool shared among the top 15 finishers. **Map** 1 B7

# Horse Racing

**Dubai Racing Club**  04 327 0077
Meydan Racecourse, Meydan City,
 Nad Al Sheba  www.dubairacingclub.com
A visit to Dubai during the winter months is not complete without experiencing race night. Dubai's top venue, Nad Al Sheba, has recently closed to make way for a new venue at Meydan City. The new racecourse opened in January 2010 and features a 60,000 seat grandstand, a five-star hotel and several restaurants. The course is the venue for the world's richest horse race, the Dubai World Cup. You can see a slightly more raw form of horseracing at Jebel Ali racecourse (04 347 4914), near The Greens.  Map 1 L7

# Motorsports

In 2009, Abu Dhabi hosted its first ever Formula 1 World Championship, held at the new Yas Island Marina Circuit in Abu Dhabi. The Formula 1 Etihad Airways Abu Dhabi Grand Prix was a high-profile three-day event which included concert performances from top acts including Beyoncé, Aerosmith and Kings of Leon. The event is set to run again from the 12-14 November in 2010, this year. The Dubai Autodrome (www.dubaiautodrome.com) is an FIA-approved circuit that hosts legs of international racing series. The Abu Dhabi Desert Challenge (www.uaedesertchallenge.com), which was previously known as the UAE Desert Challenge, is another popular event where motorbikes and 4WDs battle it out over the dunes.

# Rugby

## Dubai Rugby Sevens
The Sevens, Al Ain Road

04 321 0008
www.dubairugby7s.com

One of the biggest events in the UAE, the Dubai Rugby Sevens attracted more than 138,000 people in 2008. The two-day event is the first stop in the IRB Sevens World Series and plays host to the top 16 Sevens teams in the world. The first day of the event sees regional teams go head to head, with the international teams joining the fray for the last two days. As well as the international matches, you can also watch social, youth and women's games at the event. Tickets for the Sevens regularly sell out weeks in advance so plan early. The event has moved to a larger facility called 'The Sevens' on Al Ain Road.

# Tennis

## Dubai Tennis Championships
The Aviation Club, Dubai Tennis Stadium Al Garhoud
www.barclaysdubaitennischampionships.com

04 282 4122

The Dubai Tennis Championships takes place every February at The Aviation Club in Garhoud; it offers a great opportunity to catch some of the top players in the game at close quarters. The $1 million event is firmly established on the international tennis calendar, and features both men's and ladies' tournaments. Tickets for the later stages sell out in advance so keep an eye out for sale details – entrance to some of the earlier rounds can be bought on the day.
**Map** 5 C8 **Metro** GGICO

# Out Of Dubai

Dubai may offer everything from sun to snow but there are interesting events held just outside of the emirate should you want to venture further afield.

### Abu Dhabi Desert Challenge
050 504 8256

Empty Quarter, Abu Dhabi      www.abudhabidesertchallenge.ae

The Abu Dhabi Desert Challenge is a hot and heavy competition held in the desert around Abu Dhabi. The event sees motorbikes, 4WDs and quad bikes traverse the dunes on a five-day rally. The Desert Challenge takes place in a few different locations, including Moreeb Hill. Check the website for details of the routes – spectators are very welcome.

### Abu Dhabi Golf Championship
Abu Dhabi Golf Club,

Sas Al Nakhl Island      www.abudhabigolfchampionship.com

With $2 million in prize money and some of the biggest names in golf, the annual Abu Dhabi Golf Championship is an important event in the emirate, with more than 25,000 spectators attending the event in 2009. Every January, the European PGA Tour curtain-raiser is held at the Abu Dhabi Golf Club (02 558 8990, www.adgolfclub.com) which is renowned for its stunning course. Away from the action on the greens, there is children's entertainment, competitions and an array of food and beverage outlets, providing a fantastic family day out. The event will run from 20 to 23 January in 2011 – see website for updates.

## Al Ain Aerobatic Show
03 764 2000

Al Ain International Airport      www.alainaerobaticshow.com

This popular annual event, held every winter at Al Ain Airport, attracts thousands of spectators. The event features some incredible stunt flying with model aircrafts, helicopters, wingwalkers, gliders, and military and civilian planes. There is a festival atmosphere, with tents and displays, and children are well catered for with a play area and bouncy castles. There are a few places to get food but it may be worth packing a picnic.

## Formula 1 Etihad Airways
## Abu Dhabi Grand Prix
02 446 0384

Yas Marina Circuit, Yas Island,
Abu Dhabi          www.yasmarinacircuit.com

The inaugural Formula 1 Etihad Airways Abu Dhabi Grand Prix was held at the new Yas Island Marina Circuit in November 2009. Fans of the sport enjoyed a close view of the action on the world-class FIA sanctioned, 5.55km circuit on Yas Island. The event is set to run from 12 to 14 November this year and will again offer performances from international acts. Abu Dhabi is set to host the race for a renewable seven-year term.

## Fifa Club World Cup UAE
02 449 9955

Zayed Sports City, Abu Dhabi      www.fifa.com/clubworldcup

The Fifa Club World Cup UAE will take place at Zayed Sports City stadium and Mohammed Bin Zayed Stadium from 8 to18 December. Victors of the UAE Football League (www.uaefa. ae) will compete against six continental club champions for a prize of $16.5 million.

### Red Bull Air Race

The Corniche, Abu Dhabi                    www.redbullairrace.com

Abu Dhabi is the traditional start for the Red Bull Air Race World Series over two days each March. The Corniche is transformed into a unique racetrack with a specially built airport situated in the harbour. Spectators can view the action from the shore as the pilots race through the air just metres above the water in this competition that is both noisy and exciting. Qualifying rounds take place on the first day, while the second day sees the excitement peak with a full day of high-adrenaline racing.

### Capitala World Tennis Championship    04 408 8388

Abu Dhabi International Tennis Complex,
Zayed Sports City, Abu Dhabi           www.capitalawtc.com

Abu Dhabi's first international tennis championship was held in January 2009 and top seeds Roger Federer and Rafael Nadal competed in the event in 2010. The now annual, three-day event features family attractions for spectators, as well as a series of tennis-based activities and tournaments during the run-up to the event, including the Community Cup. Day one sees the elimination round; day two hosts the semis, and day three climaxes with the final and consolation match. Check the website for updates on the 2011 championship.

### UIM F1 Powerboat Racing World Championship

The Corniche, Abu Dhabi           www.uimpowerboating.com

The Abu Dhabi Powerboat Championship is part of the 10 stage UIM F1 Powerboat Racing World Championship. Held

Al Ain Aerobatic Show

in Abu Dhabi in December 2009, it was a joint programme by Abu Dhabi and Sharjah featuring individual championship and team events. Abu Dhabi is the first city in the Middle East to organise the UIM F1 Powerboat Race; consequently it attracts a large, appreciative audience in both Abu Dhabi and Sharjah. At this event, 20 to 24 boats representing 12 nations compete at high speed along the narrow, twisting course off the Corniche. Competitive, challenging and very entertaining, this fixture offers an interesting variation on adventure sports.

# Spas

Take some time out from the city's frenetic pace to enjoy a massage, facial or hammam – you won't have to go far to find one.

A comprehensive range of treatments is on offer in the city and you can find spas offering anything from Balinese massage, hammams and Moroccan baths, to ayurvedic treatments and hot-stone therapy in Dubai's five-star hotels.

The price of treatments varies between spas, and while basic treatments like manicures and pedicures can be cheaper in the smaller spas and salons, you will often pay a high price for more exotic treatments in the upmarket hotels. Lesser known options are just as good and often cheaper. Jumeira has several smaller spas, treatment centres and nail salons, such as Elche (p.166), that cater for those on a more modest budget. Spas will often offer set packages that combine a few treatments to make your visit more cost effective. Compare packages between spas to get the best deal – and ask about their facilities as you will often be allowed to use their, sauna, pool or Jacuzzi before or after your treatment.

Some spas only serve women, but others offer couples treatments or have separate areas for men. Grooming lounges like 1847 (p.165), which cater exclusively to men, are also increasingly popular.

## 1847

04 399 8989

Grosvenor House, Dubai Marina    www.thegroomingco.com

Considered the first dedicated 'grooming lounge' for men in the Middle East, 1847 offers manicures, professional shaves and massages in a decidedly 'manly' setting. Several of the treatments take place in private 'studies, with personal LCD TVs. There is another lounge in The Boulevard at Emirates Towers (04 330 1847) and The Walk, Jumeirah Beach Residence (04 437 0252). **Map** 2 A1 **Metro** Dubai Marina

## Akaru Spa

04 282 8578

The Aviation Club, Al Garhoud    www.akaruspa.com

The autumnal colours, natural decor, wooden fittings and glass features create a truly tranquil retreat at this Garhoud favourite. Exotic treatments range from various specialised facials and wraps to microdermabrasion. During the cooler months Akaru offers treatments on the rooftop terrace. **Map** 5 C8 **Metro** GGICO

## Amara Spa

04 602 1234

Park Hyatt Dubai, Port Saeed    www.dubai.park.hyatt.com

There is no communal changing room or wet area here, as your treatment room acts as your personal spa. After your treatments, which include, facials and Thai, Swedish and aromatherapy massages, enjoy your own private outdoor shower and relaxation area. This is one of the few places offering massage space for couples. **Map** 5 C7 **Metro** GGICO

### Assawan Spa & Health Club

04 301 7338

Burj Al Arab, Umm Suqeim          www.burj-al-arab.com

The Assawan Spa is situated on the 18th floor of the breathtaking Burj Al Arab. Unsurprisingly, it's an elaborate spot with a mosaic-covered ceiling, ornately tiled corridors and the personal service is excellent. The spa has female-only and mixed environments, including a gym with studios (where you can take part in everything from yoga to aerobics), saunas, steam rooms, plunge pools and two infinity pools looking out over the Arabian Gulf.

**Map** 2 D1 **Metro** Mall of the Emirates

### Cleopatra's Spa

04 324 7700

Pyramids, Wafi, Umm Hurair          www.wafi.com

Cleopatra's Spa may not have the grand entrance that some hotel spas share, but what it lacks in ostentation it makes up for in occasion. The relaxation area is an ancient Egyptian affair with drapes, silk cushions and majlis-style seats. The spa menu should satisfy all, with massages and facials, body wraps and anti-ageing treatments. Book a package to get a pool pass that allows you to float around the 'lazy river' in the tree-shaded pool area.  **Map** 5 A7  **Metro** Healthcare City

### Elche

04 349 4942

Nr Jumeirah Plaza, St 10, Villa 42, Jumeira          www.elche.ae

Elche utilises the healing potential of herbs, fruit and flowers in its modern scientific methods. Its skincare products are refreshingly fragrant and have a regenerative effect. Set in a walled garden this elegant retreat is warm and peaceful, with

Akaru Spa

the entire experience tailored to the individual. Not only are you given an in-depth analysis by one of the professional therapists, but you will also receive a client evaluation at the end of your treatment and can even have your makeup done by a professional. **Map** 1 M3 **Metro** Al Jafiliya

## The Grand Spa

04 317 1234

Grand Hyatt Dubai, Umm Hurair    www.dubai.grand.hyatt.com

Although this is a moderately sized spa, its atmosphere and attention to detail is spot on. The changing room and adjacent relaxation area are lit by rows of candles and the wet area (which houses a Jacuzzi, plunge pool, sauna, steam room and spacious showers) is peppered with rose petals. The spa's treatment rooms are medium in size but very comfortable. A broad range of treatments are available, from facials designed to help preserve youthfulness, to massages using essential

oils. Fusion packages combining massages, body, hand or feet treatments, facials and pilates or circuit training are also available. **Map** 5 A8 **Metro** Healthcare City

### Heavenly Spa    04 399 4141

The Westin Dubai Mina Seyahi Beach
  Resort & Marina, Al Sufouh    www.starwoodhotels.com

Similar to other luxury spas in the immediate area, the service here leaves nothing to be desired. The contemporary decor still manages to feel warm and inviting, helping to clear your mind for the gorgeous treatments that await, which includes a fabulous four-handed Heavenly Massage.
**Map** 2 B1 **Metro** Nakheel

### Man/Age    04 435 5780

Rimal 1, The Walk, Jumeirah Beach Residence,
  Dubai Marina    www.managespa.com

This luxury men's spa offers male grooming including haircuts and shaving, manicures, massages and facials. It also has a Moroccan bath. Six month and yearly memberships are available. A second branch is located in Media City (04 437 0868). **Map** 2 A1 **Metro** Dubai Marina

### Mandara Spa    04 501 8270

The Monarch Dubai,
  Trade Centre    www.themonarchdubai.com

Although one of the newest additions to Dubai's luxury spa scene, Mandara Spa has an established feel. The epicentre of the spa is a circular, cocoon-like chamber which contains

Mandara Spa

a grand Jacuzzi pool, and from here you'll find your way to the communal changing room, sauna, steam room and atmospheric treatment rooms. Many of the body therapies on offer start with a foot washing ritual, and the spa's experience is evident – nowhere more so than in the four-hands massage which is executed with expert synchronicity.

**Map** 3 D1 **Metro** World Trade Centre

## One&Only Spa                    04 315 2140

One&Only Royal Mirage,
Al Sufouh                    www.oneandonlyresorts.com

The emphasis in this serene setting is on understated decor, with plenty of neutral colours and natural light. The relaxation room is a haven of tranquillity and an ideal spot to savour the sensations after your treatment. Its speciality is the 'canyon love stone therapy', an energy-balancing massage using

warm and cool stones. The moonlight-charged stones are placed on specific points around the body, and then used to massage the skin. Only Givenchy products are used in this spa. **Map** 2 B1 **Metro** Nakheel

### Oriental Hammam
04 315 2130

One&Only Royal Mirage,
Al Sufouh                                 www.oneandonlyroyalmirage.com

This is the ultimate in Arabian luxury. The surroundings are elegant but not overly opulent, with a warm traditional feel. The hammam and spa is an impressive area with mosaic-covered arches and intricate carvings on the high domes. The 50 minute treatment involves being bathed, steamed, and washed with traditional black soap. It may sound invasive, but it is a wonderfully invigorating treatment.

**Map** 2 B1 **Metro** Nakheel

### SensAsia Urban Spa
04 349 8850

The Village, Jumeira                          www.sensasiaspas.com

Sensasia may not have all the trimmings of some five-star spas, but what it lacks in the way of plunge pools and Jacuzzis it makes up for in the 60+ minutes you spend in bliss. Enjoy the relaxing touches you would expect from an Asian-inspired spa, from candles and bamboo in the post-treatment lounge to a menu that will get your senses salivating. The hot-stone massage is sensational. This spa is not spacious but with treatments from Bali, Thailand and Japan, space is of little concern. A second branch is located on The Palm, Jumeirah (04 422 7115). **Map** 1 M3 **Metro** Al Jafiliya

## The Spa At The Address Downtown Dubai

04 436 8751

The Address Downtown Dubai,
  Downtown Dubai

www.theaddress.com

You step into total relaxation the moment you arrive at this spa, thanks to muted decor, ambient music, and a refreshing drink on arrival. The Spa has five treatment rooms for women, four for men, a couple's room, and a range of treatments including facials, massages and wraps using ESPA products. Relax on heated beds while the therapist performs your treatment after a skin analysis, and then take some time to enjoy the beautiful views over the Downtown area.

**Map** 3 B3 **Metro** Burj Khalifa/Dubai Mall

## The Spa At The Atlantis

04 426 1020

Atlantis The Palm,
  Palm Jumeirah

www.atlantisthepalm.com

From the minute you walk into The Spa's boutique area (where you can sample a wide range of products and load up on girly goodies) till the end of your treatment,

### Nail Bars

You are never too far from a perfect pedi in Dubai – the city's nail bars are pampering havens where you can enjoy basic treatments and massages in style. You will find at least one nail bar in each of the malls, and popular salons NStyle Nail Lounge (www.nstyleintl.com) and N.Bar (www.thegroomingco.com) have several locations. Also try Zen Beauty Lounge (04 434 3017, www.zenbeautylounge.com) and Tips & Toes (www.tipsntoeshaven.com).

Spas

when you're sipping green tea in the relaxation lounge, it's a heavenly experience. Even though it has 27 treatment rooms, it doesn't feel too big; perhaps because of the personal touch. Whether you choose a massage, a facial, a Bastien Gonzalez manicure, or one of the delectable Spa Journeys, your therapist has one clear focus: you. Highly recommended.
**Map** 1 D1 **Metro** Nakheel

### The Spa At The Palace

04 428 7888

The Palace – The Old Town,
Downtown Dubai                 www.thepalace-dubai.com

This spa is all about beauty and relaxation. There are separate areas where men and women can enjoy a massage, a tanning salon, a hammam, outdoor heated pool and sauna. Monsoon showers and hydrobaths wash away stress and beauty treatments using Carita products provide generous pampering. Consultants are available for personal programmes. **Map** 3 B2 **Metro** Burj Khalifa/Dubai Mall

### The Spa At Shangri-La

04 343 8888

Shangri-La Hotel, Trade Centre        www.shangri-la.com

This spa offers a holistic approach to healing, featuring traditional Asian treatments. The signature 'chi balance' massage is 50 minutes of blissful stimulation and relaxation. The health club includes a rooftop pool, tennis courts, a squash court and a gym. Relaxation facilities are extensive, with a salon, barber, juice bar and boutique. The minimalist surroundings and the communal areas lean more towards fitness club than spa. **Map** 3 C1 **Metro** Financial Centre

## Spa at The Ritz-Carlton, Dubai

04 318 6184

The Ritz-Carlton, Dubai, Dubai Marina    www.ritz-carlton.com

The opulence of the Ritz-Carlton quietly asserts itself amid the brash and trendy spots that dominate Dubai's beachfront. The Ritz-Carlton's spa, a tranquil retreat, is very much in keeping with the hotel's character. The treatment rooms are lit by candles, showing flickers of the muted tones with wood and natural stone finishes. Guests are encouraged to arrive early for their appointments to enjoy the spa's facilities – a dry sauna, eucalyptus steam room, whirlpool and relaxation room – to ready themselves for a massage, facial or body ritual from the extensive menu. **Map** 2 A1 **Metro** Dubai Marina

## Taj Spa

04 211 3101

Taj Palace Hotel, Deira    www.tajhotels.com

This is a relaxing and tranquil spa with a romantic atmosphere. The therapists concentrate on the body as well as the mind and methods are based on the ancient science of ayurveda (fused with modern technology). The changing rooms have a sauna and steam room, while the relaxation area is spacious with sink-in sofas and armchairs.

**Map** 5 C5 **Metro** Al Rigga

## Talise Spa

04 366 6818

Madinat Jumeirah, Umm Suqeim    www.jumeirah.com

On arrival, Talise's attentive staff will greet you and whisk you away to the changing rooms to start your treatments. You can, however, enjoy the spa's other facilities including sauna, steam rooms and plunge pools before or after your treatment. The treatment list is one of the most extensive in Dubai, ranging from traditional massages to more unusual options such as flower therapy. **Map** 2 D1 **Metro** Mall of the Emirates

### Timeless Spa
04 319 4000

Dubai Mariott Harbour Hotel & Suites,
 Dubai Marina
www.marriott.com

Spend a few minutes sipping ginger tea in the relaxation area, or use the sauna, steam room and Jacuzzi before your treatments in this Asian-inspired spa. There are separate areas for men and women, each with softly lit treatment rooms and ambient music. A comprehensive range of treatments are offered using Sodashi and Babor products; choose from sports massages, facials or a massage used for Hawaiian royalty. For head-to-toe pampering try the 90 minute Timeless Traditions signature body treatment for Dhs.600 which uses date extract and includes a magnificent Swedish massage. **Map** 2 A1 **Metro** Dubai Marina

### Willow Stream Spa
04 311 8800

Fairmont Dubai, Trade Centre
www.fairmont.com

In keeping with the eclectic decor of The Fairmont, Willow Stream is decorated in a luxurious Greco-Roman style. There is a selection of top-to-toe spa and beauty treatments using Aromatherapy Associates product lines. Before or after your treatment, you can use the fitness centre, the outdoor swimming pools or simply relax with a herbal tea. **Map** 3 D1 **Metro** World Trade Centre

Willow Stream Spa & Health Club

# Shopping

# Do Buy

**With souks, boutiques and mammoth malls at every turn, you won't have any problems spending your holiday money in Dubai.**

Dubai provides many opportunities to indulge in a shopping spree: it is either a shopaholic's dream or nightmare, depending on who's paying the bill. Dubai's malls (p.196) are gleaming hubs of trade filled with a mix of international high street brands and designer names. Most people head to the malls as their first stop, but it is also worth checking out some of Dubai's independent shops (p.212).

Practicality plays a large part in mall culture, and during the hotter months the malls are oases of cool in the sweltering city – somewhere to walk, shop, eat and be entertained – where you can escape the soaring heat for a few hours. From the smaller community shopping centres to the mega malls that have changed the skyline, shopping opportunities are everywhere. And with most shops open until at least 22:00 every night, and some until midnight at the weekends, there's plenty of time to browse. The popularity of the malls is evident from the crowds that they pull, particularly at the weekends, and it takes a dedicated shopper to tackle them on a Friday evening.

Souks (p.188) provide a slightly more original way to shop; they often hold a broad range of items, including souvenirs and traditional gifts, and you are able to bargain with traders to get a good price.

Saks Fifth Avenue

While prices for most items are comparable to elsewhere in the world, there are not many places that can beat Dubai's range and frequency of sales.

There are several places to buy carpets (p.183) and gold jewellery (p.184), but you'll need to bargain hard to get a good price. Electronics can be cheaper than they are the UK or US, and Dubai is the world's leading re-exporter of gold. For most items, there is enough choice to find something to fit any budget, from the streets of Karama (p.191) with its fake designer goods, to the shops in the malls (p.196) that sell the real thing. For the lowdown on where to find your essential Dubai buys, see p.182.

# Sizing

Figuring out your size is fairly straightforward. International sizes are often printed on garment labels or the store will usually have a conversion chart on display. Otherwise, a UK size is always two higher than a US size (so a UK 10 is a US 6). To convert European sizes into US sizes, subtract 32 (so a European 38 is actually a US 6). To convert European sizes into UK sizes, a 38 is roughly a 10. As for shoes, a woman's UK 6 is a European 39 or US 8.5 and a men's UK 10 is a European 44 or a US 10.5. If in doubt, ask for help.

# Bargaining

Bargaining is still common practice in the souks and shopping areas of the UAE; you'll need to give it a go to get the best prices. Before you take the plunge, try to get an idea of prices from a few shops, as there can often be a significant difference. Once you've decided how much you are willing to spend, offer an initial bid that is roughly around half that price. Stay laidback and vaguely disinterested. When your initial offer is rejected (and it will be), keep going until you reach an agreement or until you have reached your limit. If the price isn't right, say so and walk out – the vendor will often follow and suggest a compromise price. The more you buy, the better the discount. When the price is agreed, it is considered bad form to back out of the sale.

While common in souks, bargaining isn't commonly accepted in malls and independent shops. However, use your discretion, as some shops such as jewellery stores, smaller electronics stores and eyewear optical centres do operate a set discount system and the price shown may be 'before discount'. Ask whether there is a discount on the marked price and you may end up with a bargain.

## Shipping

The large number of international and local shipping and courier agencies makes transporting anything from a coffee pot to a car feasible. Both air and sea freight are available; air freight is faster but more expensive and not really suitable for large or heavy objects, whereas sea freight may take several weeks to arrive but it is cheaper and, as it is possible to rent containers, size and weight are not as much of an issue. With so many companies to choose from, it is worth getting a few quotes and finding out what will happen when the goods arrive; some offer no services at the destination while others, usually the bigger ones, will clear customs and deliver right to the door. For smaller items, or those that have to be delivered quickly, air freight is better, and the items can be tracked. Empost (600 56 5555) offers both local and international courier and air freight services at competitive prices.

### Mall Eats

Dubai has some fantastic cafes and restaurants in its malls. The Lime Tree Café (p.262) at Ibn Battuta Mall, Aprés (p.245) and Almaz by Momo at Mall of the Emirates, Organic Foods & Cafe in The Dubai Mall, More Café (p.242) at Mirdif City Centre and Shoo Fee Ma Fee (p.278) at Souk Madinat Jumeirah should get you ready for more retail.

# Where To Go For...

## Art

The art scene in Dubai, quiet for so long, is now enjoying rapid growth. There are galleries and exhibitions displaying traditional and contemporary art by Arabic and international artists working in a range of media. The Majlis Gallery (04 353 6233, www.themajlisgallery.com), located in a traditional windtower house, is a great venue for fine art, handmade glass, pottery and other unusual pieces. For cutting edge art, check out Five Green (04 336 4100, www.fivegreen.com), Opera Gallery (04 323 0909, www.operagallery.com) or XVA Gallery (04 353 5383, www.xvagallery.com), while The Art Source (04 285 6972, www.theartsource.ae) in Rashidiya stocks a range of original artwork – a framing service is also offered. You can find information on art auctions, as well as information on art fairs and gallery openings, at www.artinthecity.com.

Souk Madinat Jumeirah has the largest concentration of boutiques selling art, glass and photographs, both originals and reproductions. Many of the galleries and showrooms have a framing service or can recommend one. There are some excellent framing shops on Plant Street in Satwa (map 1 N4) and in Karama Market (map 5 A4).

## An Arabian Shopping Experience

There are a few places in Dubai where you can sidestep the glitzy mall experience and enjoy more authentic Arabian-style shopping. The Bastakiya area has a bohemian vibe and its narrow walkways, traditional windtowers and courtyards provide the perfect setting for the Bastaflea market (p.178). Souk Madinat Jumeirah's (p.193) walkways are a great place to shop for jewellery, photography and art in various mediums, while Souk Al Bahar (p.193) has some quirky boutiques and furniture stores selling traditional items. Wafi's underground marketplace, Khan Murjan (p.192), houses 150 stalls underneath its spectacular stained glass ceiling. Trade Routes, inside Dubai Festival City (p.198), is another modern take on traditional Arabian souks. Each area holds a broad range of shops as well as several restaurants should you need to refuel after you shop.

## Carpets

Carpets are one of the region's signature items, although they tend to be imported from Iran, Turkey and Pakistan. The price of a piece depends on a number of factors: its origin, the material used, the

## Fake Goods

The consumer protection department of the Dubai Department of Economic Development (www.dubaided.gov.ae) has launched a crackdown on the sale of counterfeit goods; however, the sale of such items is still very common in Dubai. If it has a logo, then you'll be able to find a 'genuine copy' version of it in Karama (p.191). The quality of goods varies, with some items being almost indistinguishable from the originals, and others being hilariously bad imitations. Inspect items properly to ensure you are buying the genuine article and not a very good fake.

number of knots, and whether or not it is hand-made. The most expensive carpets are usually those handmade with silk in Iran. The higher the quality, the neater the back, so turn the carpets over – if the pattern is clearly depicted and the knots are all neat, the carpet is of higher quality than those that are indistinct. Try to do some research so that you have a basic idea of what you are looking for before you go, just in case you happen to meet an unscrupulous carpet dealer. Fortunately, most will happily explain the differences between the rugs and share their extensive knowledge.

Ask to see a selection of various carpets and get a feel for the differences between handmade or machine-made silk, wool or blend carpets. Prices range from a few hundred to tens of thousands of dirhams. It is always worth bargaining to get a better price. To find the perfect piece head to Fabindia (Al Mankhool Road, Bur Dubai, 04 398 9633), the Pride of Kashmir (04 368 6110) in Souk Madinat Jumeirah (p.193) and Mercato (p.204), or Persian Carpet House (04 332 1161) in the Crowne Plaza. There's also a good collection of places in Deira – National Iranian Carpets (04 368 6002), Kashmir Gallery (04 222 5271) and Total Arts (04 228 2888) – and in Souk Al Bahar (p.193) in Downtown Dubai.

# Gold

Gold is notably cheaper in the UAE than in Europe, making it a popular souvenir and a main attraction for many visitors. Dubai is the world's leading re-exporter of gold and you'll find a jeweller in even the smallest of malls. It is available in 18, 21, 22 and 24 carats and is sold according to the international gold rate. This means that, for an identical piece, whether you buy it in Mall of the Emirates (p.203) or in the Gold Souk (p.190), there should be very little difference in price. You should do your research before buying anything, especially if you decide to get a piece custom-made to a design, such as a necklace with your name in Arabic. Of course, don't forget to bargain.

Many of the world's finest jewellery stores have outlets in Dubai. Both Cartier and Tiffany have numerous branches throughout the city. Simply asking for a discount, even in these upmarket retailers, can get good results. You'll find a large selection of outlets, most of which are open to bargaining, in the Gold & Diamond Park (04 347 7788) at Interchange Four on Sheikh Zayed Road, and this venue offers a slightly cooler, less frenetic shopping experience than the Gold Souk.

## Souvenirs

There is the usual selection of tacky souvenirs available in Dubai, but an equally impressive range of tasteful items are much more worthy of your money. Hand-carved wooden trinket boxes, sometimes filled with traditional oudh (a kind of incense) are popular, as are beaded wall hangings from the Textile Souk (p.195), khanjars (traditional Arabic daggers), pashminas and keffiyeh headscarves, embroidered slippers, hand-woven carpets and shisha pipes. For the ultimate in Arabian kitsch, pick up a gaudy mosque alarm clock that wakes you up with the sound of the call to prayer – it won't win you any style awards, but you'll probably be the only person on your street that has one. Good places to hunt for souvenirs include Souk Madinat Jumeirah (p.193) and Karama (p.191).

# Tailoring

If you're in town for longer than a week, it is a great opportunity to get some garments made. Tailors can be found in most areas, but the area around Dubai Museum (p.83) in Bur Dubai, or Plant Street in Satwa (p.126), are good places to start. A good tailor will be able to make a garment from scratch (rather than just make alterations), either from a photo or diagram, or by copying an existing item. If they don't get the garment spot on, they will happily make the necessary alterations.

Dream Girl Tailors (04 349 5445) in Satwa has a huge followings; it is great for everything from taking up trousers to making ball gowns. Skirts cost around Dhs.80 and dresses from around Dhs.125, depending on the complexity of the pattern. Dream Boy (04 352 1840), in Meena Bazaar, is good for shirts and suits, as is Whistle and Flute (04 342 9229); shirts usually start from Dhs.85 and suits from around Dhs.1,000. One of Dubai's most highly regarded tailors is Kachins (04 352 1386), where you may pay a little extra for a suit or shirt, but the fabric and cut will be worth it. Santoba Tailors (04 393 1234), near Choithrams in Meena Bazaar, is another great option. Its tailors will design, copy, or alter suits, dresses and anything else you can think up – it specialises in European designs and slick shirts and suits.

Clockwise from top left: Al Faheidi Street, Karama Market, Al Dhiyafah Street

# Souks & Markets

**If you want to add a slice of cultural indulgence to your shopping list, head to the souks where you'll find bargains amid the bustle.**

There are a number of souks and markets in Dubai. The souks are the traditional trading areas, some more formally demarcated than others. In keeping with tradition, bargaining is expected and cash gives the best leverage.

The Gold, Spice and Textile Souks line either side of the creek, but parking is limited, so if possible it is better to go to these areas by taxi or, if you are visiting all three, park on one side of the creek and take an abra (p.63) to the other side.

Western-style markets are becoming more popular: they are usually based around crafts and are often seasonal. The Covent Garden Market (p.189) is set up along The Walk, JBR, during the cooler months, and Bastaflea, a market near the XVA Gallery (p.85), runs on Saturdays between 10:00 and 19:00. Both are great launch pads for local talents, with artists, jewellers and other crafty types displaying their wares.

Global Village (www.globalvillage.ae), on the Emirates Road near Arabian Ranches (Map 1 E9), is a huge collection of stalls, food and entertainment from all over the world. It runs from November to February and is a good spot to pick up everything from Chinese lanterns to honey from Yemen. Organised by country, you can spend hours exploring the wares before enjoying a unique range of dishes in the international foodcourt. Just don't overdo dinner before getting on the fairground rides. Global Village is open from16:00 to midnight, Saturday to Wednesday, and until 01:00 on Thursday and Friday. Entrance costs Dhs.10 and is free for children under 2 years old.

# Covent Garden Market

The vibrancy of this street market comes from its street entertainers, open stalls and morning strollers along Jumeirah Beach Residence's cobbled beachfront promenade. You can pick up canvas or watercolour paintings from emerging artists for a rock bottom price. You will also find stalls selling fashion items, handmade jewellery, confectionary and kids' toys. The market is located in the Rimal sector of The Walk, Jumeirah Beach Residence on Wednesdays and Thursdays 17:00 till midnight and Fridays and Saturdays 10:00 to 21:00. **Map** 2 A1 **Metro** Dubai Marina

# Dubai Flea Market

This flea market is a great place to take advantage of Dubai's transient population. As people pack up and move on, an escapee's excess baggage could become a bargain hunter's treasure. For the Dhs.3 entry fee into Al Safa Park or Dhs.5 fee into Al Mamzar Beach Park, you can peruse the stalls covered with furniture, books, clothing and a broad range of unwanted items and homemade crafts. The Dubai Flea Market (www. dubai-fleamarket.com) is set up on the first Saturday of every month at Al Safa Park and every third Saturday at Al Mamzar Beach Park. A new market, the Dubai Designer Market (www.

dubaidesignermarket.com), has been introduced on the second Saturday of every month in the Beach Park Plaza. It is free to enter and you can pick up genuine second-hand luxury goods – check the website for the schedule.
**Map** 3 A1 **Metro** Business Bay

# Electronics Souk, Bur Dubai

At the heart of Bur Dubai's traditional shopping area, and bordering the Textile Souk (p.195), Al Fahidi Street is home to Dubai's electronics souk. A great place to wander round in the cooler evenings, it's perfect for a bit of local colour and some great shopping. This area is always busy but it really comes to life at night – if you're unsure whether you're in the right place, just head for the neon lights. Prices are negotiable and competitive but the vendors know the value of what they're selling. Don't make your purchases at the first shop you go into; rather, take the time to look around at the range and prices available. Although goods are often cheaper here, if you are making a big purchase, it may be worth paying that a bit extra at major retailer, so that you have more security if something goes wrong.  **Map** 5 B2 **Metro** Al Ghubaiba

# Gold Souk

This is Dubai's best-known souk and a must-do for every visitor. It's a good place to buy customised jewellery for unique souvenirs and gifts at a reasonable price.

On the Deira side of the creek, the meandering lanes are lined with shops selling gold, silver, pearls and precious stones. These can be bought as they are, or in a variety of settings so this is definitely a place to try your bargaining skills – let the vendor offer you the best discount to get the ball rolling. Gold is sold by weight according to the daily international price and so will be much the same as in the shops in malls – the price of the workmanship is where you will have more bargaining power. Most of the outlets operate split shifts, so try not to visit between 13:00 and 16:00 as many will be closed.

The Gold Souk is always busy, and it is shaded, but there is added sparkle when you visit in the evenings as the lights reflect on the gold and gems. For a comprehensive list of jewellers in Dubai, see www.dubaigoldsouk.com.
**Map** 5 C2 **Metro** Al Ras

# Karama Complex

Karama is one of the older residential districts in Dubai, and it has a big shopping area that is one of the best places to find a bargain. The best spot is the Karama Complex, a long street running through the middle of the district that is lined by shops on both sides. The area is best known for bargain clothing, sports goods, gifts and souvenirs, and it is notorious for being the hotbed of counterfeit items in Dubai. As you wander round, you will be offered 'copy watches, copy bags' with every step, and if you show any interest you will be whisked into a back room to view the goods. If you're not interested, a simple 'no thank you' will suffice, or even just ignore the vendor completely – it may seem rude, but sometimes it's the only way to cope with the incessant invitations to view counterfeit items. Two of the most popular shops are Blue Marine and Green Eye, while the imaginatively named Asda is around the corner, and offers high quality handbags and accessories crammed into two floors. It's pretty claustrophobic but the range is excellent.

There's a huge range of T-shirts, shoes, shorts and sunglasses at very reasonable prices in Karama. There are several shops selling gifts and souvenirs, from toy camels to mosque alarm clocks and stuffed scorpions to pashminas. Gifts Tent (04 335 4416) is one of the larger outlets and has a wide range, including every colour of pashmina imaginable. The salesmen are happy to take most of them out so you can find exactly the right shade. With loads of small, inexpensive restaurants serving a range of cuisines, you won't go hungry while pounding the streets of Karama. Try Chef Lanka (04 335 3050), Aryaas (04 335 5776) or Saravana Bhavan (p.276). **Map** 5 A5 **Metro** Al Karama

# Khan Murjan

For something a little different, head to Wafi's underground souk. Khan Murjan's magnificent stained glass ceiling (which stretches 64 metres) and long curved arches help make this an atmospheric place to shop. The souk features over 150 stalls selling jewellery, antiques, Arabic perfume and souvenirs. It is particularly good if you wish to spice up your home with traditional arts and crafts; there are workshops where artisans can create various bits of arts and crafts on site. In the centre of the souk, you'll find an open air marble courtyard which houses the highly recommended Khan Murjan Restaurant (04 324 4555). **Map** 5 A7 **Metro** Healthcare City

# Souk Al Bahar

While this isn't a souk in the conventional sense, Souk Al Bahar, in Downtown Dubai, is an Arabian-style mall similar to the souk at Madinat Jumeirah (p.193). Although many of the outlets serve the tourist market, there are shops for the more discerning shopper. Designer style can be found at Roccobarocco (04 361 9015) and Kitsch Boutique (04 367 4504), with Indian designer labels at Samsaara and Manish Malhotra. For exclusive beachwear, head to Pain de Sucre (04 420 0142) or vogue swimwear chain Vilebrequin (04 420 0152), and pick up a pair of famously comfortable flip-flops at the Havaianas store (04 420 0150). Marina Exotic Home Interiors (800 4360) sells contemporary home furnishings, or try Pride of Kashmir (04 420 3606), Fortix (04 420 3680) or Emad Carpet Trading (04 368 9576) for a more Arabian look. Sadek Music (04 367 4530) has a wide array of eastern and western instruments.

There are also several food outlets in the souk; you can grab light bites at Dean & Deluca and Shakespeare & Co. or something heartier at Margaux and the Rivington Grill. Hive Lounge Bar & Restaurant and Left Bank (p.298) are perfect for a post-shop cool down.

**Map** 3 B2 **Metro** Burj Khalifa/Dubai Mall

# Souk Madinat Jumeirah

Souk Madinat Jumeirah is a recreation of a traditional souk, complete with narrow alleyways, authentic architecture and motorised abras. The blend of outlets is unlike anywhere else in Dubai, with boutique shops, galleries, cafes, restaurants and bars. The layout can be a little confusing; there are maps throughout and the main features are signposted. If you're really lost, staff will happily direct you.

The souk is home to a concentration of art boutiques, including Gallery One which sells photos with a local flavour (04 368 6055) and Spirit Of Art Gallery (04 368 6207). The stalls in the outside areas sell souvenirs, some tasteful and some tacky. For holiday clobber, eye-catching but expensive swimming gear can be found at Vilebrequin (04 368 6531), Rodeo Drive (04 368 6568) and Tommy Bahama (04 368 6031).

There are more than 20 waterfront cafes, bars and restaurants to choose from, including some of Dubai's hottest night spots: Left Bank (p.298), Shoo Fee Ma Fee (p.278), Jambase (p.298) and Bar Zar (p.291) to name a few. There's also the impressive Madinat Theatre (www.madinattheatre. com) which sees international and regional artists perform everything from ballet to comedy.
**Map** 2 D1 **Metro** Mall of the Emirates

# Spice Souk

With its narrow streets and exotic aromas, a wander through the Spice Souk, next to the Gold Souk, is a great way to get a feel for the way the city used to be. Most of the stalls sell the same ranges and the vendors are usually happy to advise on the types of spices and their uses. You may even be able to pick up some saffron at a bargain price. The shops operate split shifts, but there is more bustle in the evenings.
**Map** 5 B2 **Metro** Al Ghubaiba

Textile Souk

# Textile Souk

The Textile Souk in Bur Dubai is stocked with every fabric and colour imaginable. Textiles are imported from all over the world, with many of the more elaborate coming from the Indian subcontinent and the Far East. There are silks and satins in an amazing array of colours and patterns, velvets and intricately embroidered fabrics. Basic cottons can sometimes be harder to find but you can always try Satwa (p.126). Prices are negotiable and there are often sales, particularly around the major holidays of Eid and Diwali, and the shopping festivals. It is worth having a look in a few shops before parting with your cash as stock and prices vary considerably. The mornings tend to be a more relaxed time to browse.

Nearby, Meena Bazaar is the area that most taxi drivers head for if you ask for the Textile Souk. It has an impressive number of fabric stores. Rivoli Textiles (04 335 0075) has good selection. Be sure to barter. **Map** 5 B2 **Metro** Al Ghubaiba

# Shopping Malls

**More than merely shopping destinations, Dubai's malls are epicentres of activity, with eating, drinking and even skiing on offer.**

### BurJuman

04 352 0222

Sheikh Khalifa Bin Zayed Rd, Bur Dubai    www.burjuman.com

BurJuman is renowned for its blend of designer and high-street brands attracting many a well-heeled shopper. There are enough designer shops to keep even the most dedicated fashionista happy, including Shanghai Tang, Hermes, Fendi and Christian Dior. The mall houses many famous brands, such as Gap, Polo Ralph Lauren and Escada, as well as some interesting smaller shops and legendary New York store Saks Fifth Avenue. For everyday fashion, Massimo Dutti and Zara lead the way.

The outlets within the mall are a mixture of clothing, electronics, home decor and sports goods. There are a few independent music shops that sell a good range of CDs and DVDs, and a branch of Virgin Megastore. The two foodcourts and numerous cafes are well arranged for people watching, including the popular Pavillion Gardens on the third floor, and Paul on the ground floor, where you can dine outside during the cooler months. The mall can be accessed directly from the Dubai Metro and there is plenty of underground parking and a taxi rank just outside (this gets pretty congested after 18:00 and at weekends). **Map** 5 A4 **Metro** Khalid Bin Al Waleed

## Deira City Centre

04 295 4486

Al Ittihad Rd, Deira  www.deiracitycentre.com

A stalwart of Dubai's mall scene, this centre attracts the most cosmopolitan crowd. The three floors offer a diverse range of shops where you can find anything from a postcard to a Persian carpet. There's an 11 screen cinema, a children's entertainment centre, a jewellery court, a textiles court and an area dedicated to local furniture, gifts and souvenirs.

It's all anchored by a huge Carrefour hypermarket, Paris Gallery, Debenhams, trendy department store Iconic (p.211) and a large Magrudy's bookshop. Many high-street brands are represented, including Gap, Warehouse, Topshop, Forever 21, Next and River Island. A number of designer boutiques can be found, mostly on the top floor. The City Gate section (on the same level as carparks P2 and P3) is dominated by electronics retailers.

The mall has two foodcourts: one on the first floor, next to Magic Planet, serving mainly fastfood, and one on the second floor, featuring several good sit-down restaurants. The opening of the Deira City Centre Metro station means that it is even easier to get to and from, which is great because the taxi queues can get very long, especially during weekends and in the evenings. **Map** 5 C7 **Metro** Deira City Centre

## Dubai Festival City

800 33232

Al Rebat St, Festival City  www.festivalcentre.com

Dubai Festival City incorporates the Festival Centre and The Festival Waterfront Centre. The area features around 600 retail outlets (including 25 flagship stores) and more than 100 restaurants, including 40 alfresco dining options. The need for retail therapy can be sated by the broad range of fashion, electronics and homeware outlets spread over 2.9 million square feet of retail space. Some of the biggest names in homeware, such as The White Company (04 232 5506) and the largest IKEA (800 4532) in the UAE are featured and it is home to HyperPanda (04 232 5566), a large Plug-Ins (800 758 4467) and the largest ACE store (800 275 223) outside of North America. There is also a 25,000 square foot modern gold souk where you can peruse gold from all over the world. The mall features Brit favourite Marks & Spencer (04 206 6466), high-street brands Ted Baker (04 232 6053) and Reiss (04 232 5832) and designer stores like Marc by Marc Jacobs (04 232 6118).

It's not just shopping though; The Festival Waterfront Centre has dramatic water features and performance spaces, there is a Grand Cinema (04 232 8328) and a ten-lane bowling alley on site. You can happily spend an entire day here, dining at Romano's Macaroni Grill (04 232 6001) or Steam Sum Dim Sum (04 232 9190) before relaxing in the Belgian Beer Cafe (p.291). **Map** 1 Q7 **Metro** Emirates

### Dubai Marina Mall
04 436 1000

Dubai Marina                www.dubaimarinamall.com

Located in Dubai Marina's thriving community, and within walking distance of The Walk, Jumeirah Beach Residence (p.101), this new mall's 160 outlets offer a mix of plush designer goods and high-street regulars. Several stores are yet to open, but shops like New Look (04 399 7740), Reiss (04 399 7664), Karen Millen (04 399 7525), Ted Baker (04 399 7377) and

Accessorize (04 399 7953) anchor its offering of reasonably priced fashion. Pick up kids' items at Mamas and Papas (04 399 7807) and the Early Learning Centre (04 434 2642). There is a large foodcourt with many of the usual suspects and several restaurants, including Carluccio's (04 399 7844), TGI Fridays (04 434 2686), Gourmet Burger Kitchen (04 399 7705) and Yo! Sushi (04 399 7708). The Favourite Things Mother and Child play area (04 434 1984, www.favouritethings.com) provides plenty of entertainment for kids, and you can leave your kids there so they can enjoy supervised play while you shop. There is also a branch of Reel Cinemas showing a selection of the latest releases. Yet to open is the Gourmet Tower, which will offer world-class cuisine with waterfront views.

**Map** 2 A2 **Metro** Dubai Marina

## The Dubai Mall

800 38224 6255

Financial Centre Rd,
 Downtown Dubai                     www.thedubaimall.com

The Dubai Mall is one of the world's largest malls; it will eventually house over 1,200 stores, including 160 eateries. The huge shopping and entertainment complex houses an extensive range of stores, an Olympic size ice skating rink, a catwalk for fashion shows, an enormous aquarium, a 22 screen cinema, an indoor theme park called SEGA Republic (04 448 8484), a luxury hotel, and a children's edutainment centre called KidZania (www.kidzania.ae).

   The shopping highlights are manifold, but unique to Dubai Mall are the regional flagship stores for New York department store Bloomingdales, French department store Galleries

The Dubai Mall

LaFayette (04 339 9933), the world-renowned toy shop Hamleys (04 339 8889) and UK luxury food retailer Waitrose (04 434 0700). You'll find all of the haute couture designer brands along Fashion Avenue and there is a sprawling gold souk with over 220 gold and jewellery outlets. Inside the mall, touch-screen maps and knowledgeable staff make it easy to find what you are looking for. For a complete contrast, cross the wooden bridge over the Burj Khalifa Lake and you'll find yourself in Souk Al Bahar (p.193). The tranquility of its dimly lit passageways offers a more relaxing stop after the onslaught of the mall. **Map** 3 B2 **Metro** Burj Khalifa/Dubai Mall

### Dubai Outlet Mall                                    04 367 9600

Dubai – Al Ain Rd
   (Route 66), Dubailand               www.dubaioutletmall.com

In a city where the emphasis is on excess, it is refreshing (not only for the wallet) to find a mall dedicated to saving money. Dubai's first 'outlet' concept mall may be quite a way out of town, but bargain hunters will find it's worth the drive. Brands on offer include Marc Jacobs, Tommy Hilfiger and Nike. There are also several restaurants and cafes on site. **Map** 1 L11

### Ibn Battuta Mall                                      04 362 1900

The Gardens, Off Sheikh Zayed Rd,
   Jebel Ali                              www.ibnbattutamall.com

This mall is divided into six zones each based on a region that explorer Ibn Battuta visited in the 14th century. There are several anchor stores, including Debenhams (p.210) and Géant hypermarket (04 368 5858). Shops are loosely grouped:

China Court is dedicated to entertainment, with several restaurants and a 21 screen cinema, including the UAE's first IMAX screen. Nearby is Sharaf DG (04 368 5115), and iStyle (04 366 9797) for fans of Apple products; it also does repairs in case you dropped your iPod into the hotel pool.

The fashion conscious should head to India Court for the likes of Forever 21 (04 368 5232), H&M (04 364 9819), River Island (04 368 5961), Topshop (04 368 5948) and popular independent boutique Ginger & Lace (04 368 5109). Persia Court is styled as the lifestyle area, anchored by Debenhams (04 368 5282). The foodcourts are at either end of the mall. To reward the kids for trailing round after you, there's a Fun City in Tunisia Court. The taxi points are by the entrance to each court. **Map** 1 A4 **Metro** Ibn Battuta Mall

## Mall Of The Emirates

04 409 9000

Sheikh Zayed Rd, Exit 39,
 Int 4, Al Barsha                 www.malloftheemirates.com

Mall of the Emirates is more than a mall, it's a lifestyle destination. It houses an indoor ski slope (Ski Dubai, p.152), the Kempinski Mall of the Emirates Hotel, the Pullman Dubai Mall Of The Emirates and the Dubai Community Theatre & Arts Centre (p.226). There are more than 400 outlets selling everything from forks to high fashion. The mall has been extended to include the Fashion Dome which features a selection of new restaurants and fashion outlets including a branch of More Café (p.242), a Boutique 1 store and Sephora – there are also plenty of designer names. The mall is anchored by Carrefour hypermarket, Dubai's largest branch of

Debenhams (p.210), Harvey Nichols (p.210) and Centrepoint, which is home to Baby Shop, Home Centre, Lifestyle, Shoemart and Splash. There is also a CineStar cinema (04 341 4222) where you can enjoy a film in Gold Class, which means enormous leather armchairs and waiter service throughout. Nearby, the sizeable Magic Planet (04 341 4000) includes a bowling alley, and a myriad of games and rides. Label devotees should head for Rodeo Drive (04 340 0347) to get their fix of designer labels such as Burberry, Dolce & Gabanna, Salvatore Ferragamo, Tod's and Versace. If you're more into street chic, there are two H&M stores, a branch of Reiss (04 341 0515), and a large Zara (04 341 3171). Those looking for accessories and jewellery will love Boom & Mellow (04 341 3993). Sporty types should head straight to GO Sports (04 341 3251) for all-season apparel.

For entertainment, Virgin Megastore (04 341 4353) has a bookshop and many international magazines alongside CDs, DVDs, mobile phones and computers.

You'll need to keep your energy up to explore this large mall so it's fortunate there is a wide range of dining options, from the Swiss chalet feel of Après (p.245) to a large selection of cafes and two foodcourts. Several taxis queue up outside and you can also access the Metro directly from the mall.
**Map** 2 D2 **Metro** Mall of the Emirates

### Mercato
04 344 4161

Jumeira Rd, Jumeira    www.mercatoshoppingmall.com

Mercato is the largest mall in Jumeira, with more than 90 shops, restaurants, cafes and a cinema. As you drive along

Jumeira Road, the renaissance-style architecture really makes Mercato stand out, and, once inside, the huge glass roof provides natural light and enhances the Mediterranean feel.

The mall is anchored by Spinneys (04 349 6900), a large Virgin Megastore (04 344 6971) and Gap (04 342 0745). There is a good mix of designer boutiques and high-street brands in the mall, and shops range from the reasonably priced Pull and Bear (04 344 7214) to the more exclusive Hugo Boss (04 342 2021). For fashion try Topshop (04 344 2677), Massimo Dutti (04 344 7124) and Mango (04 344 7195).

There is a foodcourt and a number of cafes and restaurants, including French cafe Paul (04 344 3505) and Bella Donna (04 344 7701), an Italian restaurant where you can dine alfresco. The cinema and large Fun City play area (04 349 9976) should keep most of the family occupied.
**Map** 1 M3 **Metro** Burj Khalifa/Dubai Mall

### Mirdif City Centre

800 6422

Emirates Rd & Tripoli St, Mirdif          www.mirdifcitycentre.com

What makes this mall stand out from the rest? Its bright, modern interior, its mix of highstreet and designer brands, and a good few stores that don't have presence elsewhere in Dubai. The mall's highlights include large branches of Boutique 1, Debenhams, Carrefour and Topshop, as well as Dubai debutants Pottery Barn and American Eagle Outfitters. If you have kids in tow, entertainment comes in the form and Playnation (www.playnationame.com), which is an emporium of fun times with highlights that include an indoor skydiving centre, a water themed play centre, a ten-pin bowling alley an

# GOLDEN TULIP
## AL JAZIRA HOTEL & RESORT

**Experience Fun Under the Sun**

P.O.Box 26268 Abu Dhabi, UAE
T +971 2 5629100 F +971 2 5629035
info@goldentulipaljazira.com   www.goldentulipaljazira.com

edutainment centre and an arcade. Top it off with a branch of More cafe, a large carpark and well-stocked foodcourts, and this is definitely one to visit if you fancy moseying down to Mirdif. **Map** 1 R9 **Metro** Rashidiya

### The Walk, Jumeirah Beach Residence   04 435 1111
Dubai Marina                              www.thewalk.ae

While this isn't strictly a mall, and the selection is rather limited, The Walk is great for browsing and cafe culture. It is a fully pedestrianised shopping area that stretches 1.7 kilometres along the beachfront. Outlets are located either on the ground level or on the plaza level of six clusters of towers called Murjan, Sadaf, Bahar, Rimal, Amwaj and Shams. The plaza level of each cluster can be accessed from large staircases, or by the lifts at ground level and in the carpark. Several outlets have closed recently – the largest cluster is now concentrated at the Murjan end. Fashion favourite Boutique 1 (04 425 7888) is located here, as are ladies' fashion stores Tara Jarmon (04 438 0339) and Antik Batik (04 434 3080). The Style Outlet has taken over the section that used to be occupied by Saks Fifth Avenue, and now carries discounted designer clothing. In the afternoons, people congregate in the many cafes in the area – particularly popular are Le Pain Quotidien (04 437 0141) and Paul (04 437 6494), and there are plenty of restaurants to dine in come the evening. Parking is available along the beach near Bahar, or in designated areas of the Murjan carpark. Many of the shops open at 10:00 and close at 22:00.
**Map** 2 A1  **Metro** Dubai Marina

## Wafi

04 324 4555
www.wafi.com

Oud Metha Rd, Umm Hurair

Wafi is one of Dubai most exclusive malls and a popular stop for the Big Bus Company tour (p.139). The store directory reads like a who's who in design. Among its most interesting boutiques are Ginger & Lace (04 324 5699), Tigerlily (04 324 8088) and baby and maternity outfit Chocolate & Pickles (04 327 9277). Imaginarium (04 324 8055), a children's toy shop, has some great traditional toys and even a separate kid-sized door. There's a large Marks & Spencer (04 324 5145) and a branch of department store Jashanmal (04 324 4800) for a break from the likes of Versace (04 324 7333).

There are a number of cafes and restaurants in the mall, including Italian restaurant Biella (04 324 4666), where you can eat in the alfresco dining area. Wafi Gourmet (04 324 4433) is a great place to pick up freshly made Arabic dishes and a delicious selection of olives and dates. The children's entertainment area, Encounter Zone (04 324 7747), is very popular and has age-specific attractions. If you feel the need for pampering, or an evening out, head across to the Pyramids complex where there are some excellent bars and restaurants and a renowned spa (p.166).

Additions to the area include the five-star Raffles Dubai hotel (p.69), an underground carpark and 90 new shops, including UK fashion store Topshop (04 327 9929), popular LA retailer Kitson (04 324 2446) and several outlets in Khan Murjan souk (p.192). **Map** 5 A7 **Metro** Healthcare City

# Department Stores

The scope of department stores covers the full shopping spectrum, from the epitome of chic at Saks Fifth Avenue to the functionality of M&S.

## Debenhams

Various Locations                    www.debenhams.com

A stalwart of the British high street, Debenhams has four stores in Dubai: Deira City Centre (p.198), Ibn Battuta Mall (p.202), Mall of the Emirates (p.203) and The Dubai Mall (p.200). The branches all stock perfumes and cosmetics, clothing for men, women and children, and homewares. They carry the popular Designers at Debenhams range with diffusion lines from John Rocha, Betty Jackson, Jasper Conran, Matthew Williamson and Ben de Lisi. This is a good shop for swimwear all year round.

## Harvey Nichols

04 409 8888

Mall of the Emirates, Al Barsha       www.harveynichols.com

Dubai simply couldn't call itself a luxury destination without its own Harvey Nichols (the largest branch outside the UK). It contains a large selection of high-rolling fashion, food, beauty and homeware brands, as well as an intimidating selection of sunglasses. Pick up fashion treats from Jimmy Choo, Diane Von Furstenberg, Juicy Couture, Hermes and Sergio Rossi, then head to the top floor for the popular Almaz by Momo (04 409 8877), a restaurant, juice bar and shisha cafe all in one. **Map** 2 D3  **Metro** Mall of the Emirates

## Iconic

04 294 3444

Deira City Centre, Deira　　　　　　　　　　www.iconic.ae

This store screams urban style and luxury – all 70,000 square feet of it. Hidden away at one end of Deira City Centre (you can find it by the Metro entrance) the store stocks high street and designer fashion for men and women from an assortment of international brand names. It also has an electronics boutique, accessories section, cosmetics area and two restaurants. **Map** 5 C7 **Metro** Deira City Centre

## Jashanmal

Various Locations　　　　　　　　　　www.jashanmal.ae

One of Dubai's original department stores, with branches in Al Ghurair City, Mall of the Emirates and Wafi, Jashanmal is the importer for several brands including Burberry, Clarks shoes and Mexx. With books, cameras, fashion, gifts, housewares, household and kitchen appliances, and luggage, the stores are definitely worth a look.

## Marks & Spencer

Various Locations　　　　　www.marksandspencerme.com

One of the best known brands in the UK, M&S sells men's, women's and children's clothes and shoes, along with a small selection of food. It is famous for its underwear selection and has a reputation for quality. You'll also find more fashion-forward lines including Limited Collection, Per Una, and Autograph alongside the traditional styles it has been carrying for years. Branches in Wafi (p.209) and Dubai Festival City (p.198) and The Dubai Mall (p.200).

**Shopping**

**Department Stores**

### Saks Fifth Avenue

04 351 5551

BurJuman, Bur Dubai                    www.saksfifthavenue.com

Anchoring the extension to BurJuman is the second-largest Saks Fifth Avenue outside the US. The name is synonymous with style, elegance, and the good life, encapsulated on two floors of paradise for the label conscious. You'll find designers galore, including Christian Dior, Jean Paul Gaultier, Prada, Agent Provocateur and Tiffany & Co, in addition to a personalised shopping service.

**Map** 5 A4  **Metro** Khalid Bin Al Waleed

# Supermarkets & Hypermarkets

The city's large supermarkets and hypermarkets stock a good range of international products and a comprehensive range of electronics, household goods, luggage and mobile phones. Carrefour (www.carrefouruae.com) has several locations in the city, and it is the best place to buy French products (particularly good are its crusty bread and selection of French cheeses). Its stores also stock camping gear, clothes, music, DVDs and stationery. UK store Waitrose has branches in Dubai Marina Mall (04 434 2626) and The Dubai Mall (04 434 0700) and its deli counter is great for picnic items and snacks. Spinneys (www.spinneys-dubai.com) stocks a great range of imported food items.

# Independent & Noteworthy Shops

Dubai's independent scene is blossoming. Individual stores and boutiques are opening, predominantly in converted villas, all over the city. You'll find the odd store in Souk

Ibn Battuta Mall

Al Bahar (p.193) or The Walk, Jumeirah Beach Residence (p.208), but Jumeira Road in Jumeira is one of the most popular destinations.

Five Green (04 336 4100, www.fivegreen.com), is a funky independent store that can be found next to the Garden Home Center on Oud Metha Road. It's a great place to find cutting-edge fashion and art. Fabindia (04 398 9633, www.fabindia.com) has one of only two branches outside India in Dubai. A riot of bright colours and subtle hues, the clothing ranges

for men and women combine Indian and western styles. The hand-crafted fabrics, including soft furnishings, table cloths and cushion covers, will add an ethnic touch to your home.

The items at S*uce are anything but basic, but you can peruse the funky accessories, pick up quirky high-fashion, and individual pieces at this eclectic boutique in The Village mall (04 344 7270) and a new outlet in The Dubai Mall (8003 8224 6255). For cosmetics, jewellery and accessories head to high-end department store Paris Gallery (04 330 8289, www. parisgallery.com) and newly opened French department store Galeries Lafayette (04 339 9933) in Dubai Mall (p.200).

### Gold & Diamonds

**The Gold & Diamond Park (04 347 7788, www. goldanddiamondpark. com), is a great place to buy jewellery if you are more interested in buying than enjoying the souk experience. There are branches of many of the outlets that are also found in the Gold Souk (p.190) but here they are much quieter (Map 5 C2).**

Those looking for home accessories should consider THE One (04 345 6687) on Jumeira Road. A long-time favourite of Dubaians, it sells contemporary furniture, as well as more unusual one-off pieces that are often elaborate and rather over the top. Its cafe is a great spot for a break while trawling Jumeira Road. Burlesque (04 346 1616) on Al Wasl Road is an elaborate store with highly romantic furniture and plenty of floral prints. This is the place to head if you are bored with formulaic approaches to interior design and would like some stylish, but eccentric, peices to take home.

Pinky Furniture (04 422 1720, www.pinkyfurniture.com), in Al Barsha, is particularly good for buying Indian teak furniture. Italian leather furniture maker Natuzzi (04 338 0777) has its largest international branch on Sheikh Zayed Road, between Interchanges Two and Three. Contemporary Arabian prints can be found at Gallery One, which has several branches including a store in Mall of the Emirates (04 341 4488), Souk Madinat Jumeirah (04 368 6055) and The Walk, Jumeirah Beach Residence (04 423 1987).

The boho enclave of The Courtyard (www.courtyard-uae. com) in Al Quoz has funky furniture and accessories amid its art galleries. Traffic (www.viatraffic.org) is a gallery, gift shop and studio in Al Barsha that stocks fashion items, interior design pieces and small gifts. The Antiques Museum (04 347 9935), in Al Quoz, is full to the brim with everything from souvenirs (not all of them from the UAE), to furniture, pashminas and Omani silver, the prices are less than in tourist hotspots like Souk Madinat Jumeirah and wandering through its passageways and secret rooms is a treat. There are several places to buy electronics but Sharaf DG (www.sharafdg.com) is one of the more popular spots. You'll find branches of the store in several of the malls but its largest store is in Times Square Center (800 344 357). For something for the kids head to Candylicious (04 330 8700, www.candyliciousshop. com), the super-sized sweet shop in The Dubai Mall that has enough goodies to keep those with a sweet tooth grinning from ear to ear.

# Going Out

# Dine, Drink, Dance

**Celebrity chefs, world-class nightlife and plenty of grilled meat. Dubai's culinary and entertainment options will blow you away.**

Dubai's gastronomic landscape is huge and constantly growing. Celebrity chefs, cheap ethnic eateries, picturesque bars and mammoth clubs combine to form the region's most exciting nightlife. The city's varied population and ritzy reputation has produced a demand for exceptional food. Fine-dining aficionados will be impressed with the diversity, quality and abundance of first-rate restaurants, while culinary tourists can dine on authentic Arabic kebabs for lunch and fiery Pakistani curries for dinner.

Thursday and Friday nights are the big ones, with reservations required in the restaurants and international DJs in the clubs. However, during the week you'll find drinks deals across the city and all manner of dining promotions. See Brunch & Other Deals (opposite) for more information.

### The Yellow Star

The little yellow star highlights venues that merit extra praise. It could be the atmosphere, the food, the cocktails, the music or the crowd, but whatever the reason, any review that you see with the star attached is somewhere considered a bit special.

While Dubai doesn't lend itself to pub crawls by foot or evening strolls around restaurant districts, venues tend to be close together, either within a hotel, or a mall such as Souk Madinat Jumeirah (p.193), or a short taxi ride away.

Keep in mind that Dubai's licensing laws are unique. For a venue to serve alcohol, it must be attached to a hotel or a sporting facility. This means no supermarket six-packs and no wine at your independent bistro. The legal drinking age is 21, and it's best to avoid getting staggeringly drunk as it may land you behind bars. Most importantly, don't even think about getting behind the wheel of a car after drinking – Dubai maintains a strict zero tolerance stance on drunk driving. Respect the laws and you'll have nothing to worry about – Dubai certainly knows how to throw a party.

## Brunch & Other Deals

With so many venues to choose from, Dubai's restaurants and bars face stiff competition in attracting punters. As a result, there are some excellent deals on food and drink almost every day of the week. All-you-can-eat-and-drink deals abound, and some of the city's best restaurants offer time-specific deals that let diners experience exquisite creations at extreme discounts – Verre (p.284) offers a three course meal for Dhs.395, and food is half price at Teatro (p.281) if you order before 19:30. Tuesday has become the official ladies' night for several of Dubai's drinking institutions, including Double Decker (p.295) and Oeno (p.299). Check the websites of your favourite places before you make your plans as new offers are always being introduced.

The king of all Dubai deals, however, is the Friday brunch, and a lazy, drawn out, all-you-can-eat-and-drink afternoon is a must for any visitor. Many of the finest five-star hotels, including Al Qasr (p.68), Burj Al Arab (p.67), The Park Hyatt (p.69) and Jumeirah Beach Hotel (p.68) put on lavish spreads every Friday afternoon and they're almost always packed with punters. These all-you-can-eat-and-drink affairs often include unlimited champagne and food from all over the world. Of course, such luxury comes at a price – usually upwards of Dhs.350 for the premium options. If you want to indulge in daytime dining but want to save the dirhams then there are some decent cheaper options, such as Organic Foods & Cafe's Dhs.95 for adults and Dhs.65 for kids option (04 434 0577) and Pergolas (04 321 1111) in the Murooj Rotana, which offers all-you-can-eat-and-drink themed dinner buffets every night of the week.

## Double Trouble

Dubai has a number of restaurants that deserve extra credit for their stellar bars. Trader Vic's (p.282) serves some stunning cocktails, while El Malecon (p.254) and Spectrum on One (p.278) are worth a trip for the bar alone. Likewise, several of Dubai's bars, including Left Bank (p.298), Caramel (p.294) and Sho Cho's (p.300) serve food that's tasty enough to warrant a table reservation.

## Vegetarian

There are plenty of delicious local delicacies that will thrill herbivores. Rahib salad, a hot combination of aubergine and tomato, makes a great side dish when eating Lebanese food, as do tabouleh, fattouth and falafel, all served with fluffy fresh bread. What's more, the huge population of south Asians means there are plenty of authentic vegetable curries. Head to Karama (p.191) to try a veg thali, which consists of up to 10 small pots of curries, pickles and sauces into which you can dip chapatti or mix with rice. Saravana Bhavan (p.276) is an exceptionally good choice, and the experience will rarely cost you more than Dhs.12. Magnolia (p.262) in Al Qasr Hotel has won legions of fans for its decidedly gourmet vegetarian menu.

## Karaoke

The draw of the microphone and the lure of crooning embarrassment is alive and well in Dubai, and the city's best karaoke bars are tight and intimate, just as they should be. Harry Ghatto's (04 330 0000) in Emirates Towers is a favourite, Hibiki (04 209 6701) in Bur Dubai has private rooms, and It's Mirchi (04 334 4088) offers a bizarre Indian alternative, complete with plenty of curries and a multi-lingual songbook.

## Nightclubs

Massive sound systems, international DJs, incredibly diverse interiors and just enough musical variety to keep things interesting – Dubai's club scene has long been the best in the region, and it keeps getting better. House and popular R&B dominate Dubai's dancefloors, but some clubs regularly promote theme nights such as Arabic, Indian and cheesy music. Door policies differ from venue to venue. Some of the most exclusive spots, such as Cavalli Club (04 332 9260) and The 400 (04 332 4900), won't let you in unless you're on the guest list, while others like Chi@The Lodge (p.294) merely require a decent pair of shoes.

## Street Food

The shawarma is to Dubai what the hot dog is to New York. The popular snack, consisting of rolled pita bread filled with lamb or chicken carved from a rotating spit, can be found throughout the city, and tiny cafeterias serving the delicacy are around every corner. At about Dhs.3 each, they're the perfect end to a big night out or a tasty pre-club snack. Try to avoid shawarma stands that carve from tiny slabs of meat – a huge shawarma spit is a good sign that the cafeteria has a high turnover. Street-side cafeterias also squeeze and

### Shisha

It's common to see people relaxing in the evening with a shisha pipe. Shisha is a popular method of smoking tobacco with a water-filled pipe. It comes in a variety of flavours, including grape and apple. Some of the best places to try shisha in Dubai are Reem al Bawadi (p.274), and QD's at The Boardwalk (p.250).

press some of the best and least expensive fresh juices in the city.

## Arabian Experience

Aside from at Bastakiah Nights (p.248), specialist local Emirati dishes like *al machboos* or *al harees* can be hard to come by in Dubai's restaurants. However, there's plenty of opportunity to experience other Arabic cuisines.

Most of Dubai's Arabic fare hails from Lebanon and Syria. Tabouleh (chopped parsley with bulgar, tomato and herbs), fattoush (salad seasoned with sumac and topped with toasted pita), aryaas (grilled flat bread with spiced meat in the middle) and many kinds of grilled, skewered meat can be found in any Arabic restaurant and are great introductions to regional cuisine. Head to Reem Al Bawadi (p.274) for an authentic first try. For more adventurous diners, upscale Arabic eateries such as Levantine (p.260) offer menus with more exotic dishes.

For the full Arabian experience, try heading out on a desert safari (p.138) where you'll be entertained by a belly dancer, dine on a full array of Arabic delights under the stars and smoke the requisite shisha.

### All Aboard

Dinner on the creek is a must. While in town, try the five-star fare of Bateaux Dubai (04 399 4994, www. bateauxdubai.com) or Creek Cruises (04 393 9860, www. creekcruises.com) for the tourist option, that comes complete with a belly dancer.

# Entertainment

With a popular film festival, massive concerts, and a growing theatre scene, Dubai is a regional entertainment hub.

## Cinema

Dubai loves going to the movies, and the city's residents flock to the cinemas every weekend. Aside from Reel Cinemas in The Dubai Mall which occasionally shows independent films, Dubai tends to mainly show mainstream films. The biggest cinemas include a 22 screen outlet in the Dubai Mall (Reel Cinemas, 04 449 1988, www.reelcinemas.ae) and a 21 screen cinema at Ibn Battuta Shopping Mall (Grand Megaplex, www.grandcinemas.com) – the latter has the region's first IMAX screen.

Outdoor screenings have become popular in the past year and The Desert Palm (04 323 8888), Wafi (p.209), and the Dubai Polo and Equestrian Club (04 361 8111) each devotes a night to outdoor cinema.

At weekends, there are extra shows at midnight or 01:00. Cinema timings can be found in daily newspapers, or at www.explorerpublishing.com/dubai or individual cinema websites. A definite cinematic highlight is Dubai International Film Festival (p.53). The event runs for a week in December across various locations in the city and showcases an impressive mix of mainstream, world and local cinema – from shorts to full features.

## Comedy

Comedy nights in Dubai are popular with the expat crowd but events tend to be semi-regular, rather than weekly nights. The Laughter Factory organises monthly performances, with comedians from the UK's Comedy Store coming over to play various venues throughout Dubai, including Zinc (p.301) and The Aviation Club (www.aviationclub.ae). A lot of comedy is aimed at the expat crowd, so unless you're familiar with the comedian's country, you might not be laughing. Keep an eye on www.thelaughterfactory.com for details of future shows.

## Live Music

Dubai hosts a number of concerts each year, and as the city grows it attracts bigger names. Past acts include Muse, Kanye West, Sting and Robbie Williams. The bigger names usually play at outdoor venues such as the Tennis Stadium, Dubai Autodrome and the amphitheatre at Media City.

In addition to acts at the height of their fame, Dubai also plays host to a string of groups that may be past their prime, but nonetheless provide good entertainment

### Something Different

Many of the nightclubs in Bur Dubai's three and four-star hotels feature live bands that cater for a certain culture. For African music, head to the Beach Club at the Palm Beach Hotel (04 393 1999) and for a lively Filipino band try Maharlika at the President Hotel (04 334 6565).

(think Human League, Tony Hadley, Go West, Echo & The Bunnymen and Deacon Blue).

There has been a recent rise in alternative and slightly lesser-known acts coming over for some sun including Groove Armada, 2ManyDjs and Super Furry Animals. Dubai also hosts several music festivals each year focusing on rock, rhythm and world music. For more information on events in Dubai and Abu Dhabi, keep an eye on Explorer's website (www.explorerpublishing.com) which has details of events, promotions and upcoming gigs in Dubai and Abu Dhabi.

## Theatre

The theatre scene in Dubai has always been rather limited, with fans relying chiefly on touring companies and the occasional amateur dramatics performance. However, as the city grows so does its thirst for culture, and with an increase in modern facilities over the past couple of years, theatre lovers finally have something to cheer about. The Madinat Theatre (www.madinattheatre.com) hosts a variety of performances, from serious stage plays to comedies and musical performances. Cirque du Soleil has set up its massive big-top at Ibn Battuta each spring for the past few years and is always a bit hit. The Palladium (www.thepalladiumdubai.com), is located in Media City and has hosted acts from Akon to The Wiggles. Dubai Community Theatre and Arts Centre (www.ductac.org) at Mall of the Emirates provides valuable theatre space for amateur dramatics performances, as well as for smaller-scale shows which have included touring shows from Edinburgh's Fringe festival.

Dubai Community Theatre and Arts Centre

# Venue Directory

## Cafes & Restaurants

## Italian

| | | |
|---|---|---|
| | Bussola | p.250 |
| | Ronda Locatelli | p.275 |
| | Segreto | p.277 |
| | Splendido | p.279 |
| | Vivaldi | p.285 |

## Japanese

| | | |
|---|---|---|
| | Creekside | p.252 |
| | Kitsune | p.258 |
| | Mirai | p.266 |
| | Momotaro | p.266 |
| | Nobu | p.269 |
| | Okku | p.270 |
| | Sushi Sushi | p.280 |
| | tokyo@thetowers | p.282 |
| | Zuma | p.286 |

## Korean

| | | |
|---|---|---|
| | Sumibiya | p.280 |

## Latin American

| | | |
|---|---|---|
| | El Malecon | p.254 |
| | Latino House | p.260 |
| | Pachanga | p.270 |

## Lebanese

| | | |
|---|---|---|
| | Al Nafoorah | p.244 |

## Mediterranean

| | | |
|---|---|---|
| | az.u.r | p.247 |
| | Majlis Al Bahar | p.263 |
| | Villa Beach | p.285 |
| | Vu's | p.285 |

# Area Directory

## Al Barsha
**Restaurants**

## Al Karama
**Restaurants**

## Al Garhoud & Festival City
**Restaurants**

**Bars, Pubs & Clubs**

## Al Satwa
**Restaurants**

| Pars Iranian Kitchen | Nr Rydges Plaza | p.272 |
| Ravi's | Al Satwa Rd, Nr Satwa R/A | p.274 |

# Al Sufouh & Palm Jumeirah

## Restaurants

| Beach Bar & Grill | One&Only Royal Mirage | p.248 |
| Bussola | The Westin Dubai Mina Seyahi Beach Resort & Marina | p.250 |
| The Dhow | Le Meridien Mina Seyahi Beach Resort & Marina | p.252 |
| Eauzone | One&Only Royal Mirage | p.254 |
| Levantine | Atlantis The Palm | p.260 |
| Nasimi | Atlantis The Palm | p.268 |
| Nina | One&Only Royal Mirage | p.268 |
| Nobu | Atlantis The Palm | p.269 |
| Ossiano | Atlantis The Palm | p.270 |
| Ronda Locatelli | Atlantis The Palm | p.275 |
| Rostang | Atlantis The Palm | p.275 |
| Seafire | Atlantis The Palm | p.277 |
| Tagine | One&Only Royal Mirage | p.280 |
| Trader Vic's | Souk Madinat Jumeirah | p.282 |

## Bars, Pubs & Clubs

| The Agency | Souk Madinat Jumeirah | p.288 |
| Bar Zar | Souk Madinat Jumeirah | p.291 |
| Barasti | Le Meridien Mina Seyahi Beach Resort & Marina | p.291 |
| BidiBondi | Clubhouse Al Manhal, Shoreline Apartments | p.292 |
| Jambase | Souk Madinat Jumeirah | p.298 |

Verre By
  Gordon Ramsay | Hilton Dubai Creek | p.284
Vivaldi | Sheraton Dubai Creek
  Hotel & Towers | p.285

# Downtown Dubai & Sheikh Zayed Road

## Restaurants

| | | |
|---|---|---|
| Al Nafoorah | Boulevard at Emirates Towers | p.244 |
| Amwaj | Shangri-La Hotel | p.244 |
| Asado | The Palace – The Old Town | p.245 |
| The Exchange Grill | Fairmont Dubai | p.255 |
| Flavours On Two | Towers Rotana Hotel | p.256 |
| Kitsune | Fairmont Dubai | p.258 |
| Latino House | Al Murooj Rotana Hotel & Suites | p.260 |
| Margaux | Souk Al Bahar | p.264 |
| Marrakech | Shangri-La Hotel | p.265 |
| The Meat Co | Souk Al Bahar | p.265 |
| Mirai | Souk Al Bahar | p.267 |
| Momotaro | Souk Al Bahar | p.266 |
| Okku | The Monarch Dubai | p.270 |
| The Rib Room | Emirates Towers Hotel | p.275 |
| Shang Palace | Shangri-La Hotel | p.278 |
| Spectrum On One | Fairmont Dubai | p.278 |
| Teatro | Towers Rotana Hotel | p.281 |
| Thiptara | The Palace – The Old Town | p.282 |
| tokyo@thetowers | Boulevard at Emirates Towers | p.282 |
| Vu's | Emirates Towers Hotel | p.285 |

## Dubai Marina, JBR & JLT

**Restaurants**

## Oud Metha & Umm Hurair

# Restaurants & Cafes

**Dubai's culinary landscape includes everything from mountainous buffet spreads to low-key streetside snacks.**

There isn't much you can't find in Dubai when it comes to food; whether it's a quick-fix burger, super fresh fish and chips or sizzling curries, the variety is extraordinary. Dining in one of Dubai's five-star hotel resorts is a must, if only to witness the tremendous variety and quality. Bookings are not always necessary, but it is best to check as hotel guests often get first dibs on the tables and popular restaurants do fill up quickly.

Alternatively, bypass Michelin-starred options and still get fare that is both tasty and easy on the wallet. Visitors should experience some of Dubai's more modest, but certainly vibrant and atmospheric, independent Indian restaurants such as Saravana Bhavan (p.276) and popular Pakistani restaurant Ravi's (p.274). There are also several Arabic restaurants (p.225) that are worth a try. Al Mallah (opposite) on Al Dhiyafah Road in Satwa, is a popular spots for pavement dining, shawarmas and juices at very reasonable prices.

When it comes to breakfast and lunch, you can grab a bite at the delightful cafes loved by Dubai's expats such as More Café (04 283 0224, www.morecafe.biz), Shakespeare & Co. (04 331 1757), Lime Tree Cafe (p.262) and Epicure (p.254). For real cafe culture, stroll along The Walk, Jumeirah Beach Residence which offers up a wide selection of restaurants and cafes, and plenty of opportunity to people watch, along its beachfront promenade.

### Al Dawaar
Hyatt Regency Dubai, Deira
International
04 209 1234

While you may think a revolving restaurant is mere kitsch, don't be too hasty in dismissing Al Dawaar. This is a surprisingly sophisticated Arabic buffet restaurant on the 25th floor of the hotel. As you enjoy the cuisine including Japanese and Middle Eastern dishes, the slow revolution (it takes one hour and 45 minutes to do a complete turn) gives you an interesting window on this side of town.
**Map** 5 D2 **Metro** Palm Deira

### Al Mahara
Burj Al Arab, Umm Suqeim
Seafood
04 301 7600

Your visit to Al Mahara starts with a simulated submarine ride that takes you 'under the sea' to dine among the fish. 'Disembark' and you'll see the restaurant is curled around a huge aquarium. The menu is almost exclusively seafood. It's fine dining at its finest, with prices to match. Gentlemen are required to wear a jacket for dinner.
**Map** 2 D1 **Metro** Mall of the Emirates

### Al Mallah
Al Dhiyafah St, Al Satwa
Arabic
04 398 4723

Al Mallah offers great pavement dining with an excellent view of the world and his brothers cruising by in their Ferraris. The shawarmas and fruit juices are excellent, the cheese and zatar manoushi exceedingly tasty, and it has possibly the biggest and best falafel in Dubai. The incongruous 'Diana' and 'Charles' shakes are recommended. **Map** 1 N3 **Metro** Al Jafiliya

### Al Muntaha

International

Burj Al Arab, Umm Suqeim      04 301 7600

If you weren't at the top of the Burj Al Arab, with an unrivalled view of Dubai's coastline, you would be forgiven for thinking this restaurant's decor is a bit tacky considering the price tag. The menu is less surprising than the decor, with the usual suspects in a European fine-dining line-up. The food is certainly good, despite an atmosphere akin to a private members' club. **Map** 2 D2 **Metro** Mall of the Emirates

### Al Nafoorah

Lebanese

Boulevard at Emirates Towers, Trade Centre      04 319 8088

The menu at this highly rated Lebanese restaurant is extensive, with pages and pages of mezze and mains to tantalise. It's best to come in a group and share the wide selection. After dinner, you can take a stroll round The Boulevard, or sit out and enjoy shisha in front of the looming Emirates Towers. **Map** 3 D2 **Metro** Emirates Towers

### Amwaj

Seafood

Shangri-La Hotel, Trade Centre      04 405 2703

The minimal decor here cleverly depicts a marine theme yet remains refined. An immaculate sushi bar greets you, and the open kitchen allows you to watch tantalising dishes being prepared. The menu offers endless fish and seafood creations, and the vegetarian and meat choices are equally impressive, especially the foie gras. Adventurous diners should consider the tasting and set menus.
**Map** 3 C1 **Metro** Financial Centre

Al Mallah

### Après
European

Mall Of The Emirates, Al Barsha
04 341 2575

This cosy alpine ski lodge has a comfortable bar area and an unrivalled view of the slope. The varied menu offers wholesome fare including steaks, fondue and excellent pizzas. During the day it's great for families, but at night the laidback vibe and wide-ranging cocktail list encourages both chilling and partying. **Map** 2 D3 **Metro** Mall of the Emirates

### Asado
Steakhouse

The Palace – The Old Town, Downtown Dubai
04 428 7888

A combination of moody lighting, passionate music, a killer location and a meat lovers' dream menu cement Asado's top

steakhouse position. Excellent meat and an enormous wine selection, with terrace views of Burj Khalifa thrown in, make this Argentinean restaurant something very special.
**Map** 3 B2  **Metro** Burj Khalifa/Dubai Mall

### Asha's
Indian
Pyramids, Wafi, Umm Hurair                    04 324 4100
Owned by Indian superstar Asha Bhosle, this Dubai favourite offers a memorable dining experience. Decked out in summer colours of reds, yellows, and oranges, the space features beaded curtains, low-level lighting, and intimate booths as well as an inviting terrace. The menu features a few Indian favourites plus a selection of Asha's very own signature dishes picked up on her travels.  **Map** 5 A7  **Metro** Healthcare City

### Ashiana
Indian
Sheraton Dubai Creek Hotel & Towers, Deira        04 207 1733
With empire-inspired decor and a traditional band playing authentic tunes every night, Ashiana celebrates India's colonial era. Cosy booths around the walls are the seats of choice, unless you're in a large group. The staff deserve a special mention for their swift and friendly service.
**Map** 5 C4  **Metro** Union

### Asiana Restaurant
Thai
Raffles Dubai, Umm Hurair                     04 314 9888
Feast on a host of Asian-inspired dishes (including a truly remarkable pad thai) while savouring the beautiful city

views at this atmospheric venue. With a cool, classy interior, a breathtaking balcony and fine dining at non-exorbitant prices, Asiana ticks all the right boxes.

**Map** 5 A7  **Metro** Healthcare City

## az.u.r                                                     Mediterranean

Dubai Marriott Harbour
 Hotel & Suites, Dubai Marina                         04 319 4000

az.u.r offers a range of hearty meat, fish and seafood dishes, super fresh vegetables served with simple style. The food is excellent with rich combinations of ingredients, and represents cuisine from France, Morocco, Spain and Italy. The service is knowledgeable and friendly, and there's a great Marina view from the terrace.

**Map** 2 A1  **Metro** Dubai Marina

## Bamboo Lagoon                                            Far Eastern

JW Marriott Hotel, Deira                                  04 607 7009

With a little bridge and a big crocodile, you won't forget this restaurants' decor in a hurry. The food is memorable too: there's sushi, tempura, teriyaki, curries, steaks, stir-fries, grills, seafood, rice and noodle dishes. All are equally tempting and so wonderfully presented that you'll wish you hadn't eaten that big lunch. At 21:00 a band takes to the stage and grass-skirted singers serenade diners with low-key renditions of tropical Polynesian tunes and entertaining cover versions.

**Map** 5 D5  **Metro** Abu Baker Al Siddique

### Bastakiyah Nights

Arabic

Bastakiya, Bur Dubai
04 353 7772

As you enter through heavy wooden doors you are reminded that, despite the glitzy malls and luxurious hotels, Dubai is still very much Arabia. The food is delectable. You can choose from fixed menus or the various a la carte offerings such as lamb stew and stuffed vine leaves. There's no alcohol licence but that shouldn't matter with food this good.

**Map** 5 B2 **Metro** Al Fahidi

### Beach Bar & Grill

Seafood

One&Only Royal Mirage, Al Sufouh
04 399 9999

This superb restaurant is definitely one to pull out when you want a truly romantic evening. Seafood lovers must make a trip to this opulent, intimate beach bar. Terrace tables are candle-lit, and the fresh fish is cooked simply but with style. Seafood platters to share, and surf and turf options, are available for people who simply can't pick just one dish.

**Map** 2 B1 **Metro** Nakheel

### Beachcombers

Far Eastern

Jumeirah Beach Hotel, Umm Suqeim
04 406 8999

This breezy shack has an idyllic location right on the beach with fantastic views of the Burj Al Arab. Expect excellent far eastern buffets with live cooking stations for stir-fries and noodles. The peking duck, curry hotpots and satay are highly recommended. **Map** 2 D1 **Metro** Mall of the Emirates

## Blue Elephant

Thai

Al Bustan Rotana Hotel, Al Garhoud          04 282 0000

Walking into The Blue Elephant is like travelling to Thailand without the hassle of jetlag. While sitting at bamboo tables, gazing into a lagoon and surrounded by verdant tropical greenery, the smell of orchids is evocative of exotic far eastern climates. The menu showcases an array of superb Thai food, spiced to your liking, with distinctive oriental ingredients and traditional flavours. **Map** 5 D8 **Metro** GGICO

## The Boardwalk

International

Dubai Creek Golf & Yacht Club, Port Saeed          04 295 6000

Positioned on wooden stilts over the creek, The Boardwalk's view is virtually unmatched in Dubai. The menu is varied enough to suite all tastes, the food is well prepared, and the drinks list contains a huge selection of cocktails and mocktails. Just next door sits QD's, which shares the same incredible views but concentrates more on drinks and shisha. **Map** 5 C8 **Metro** Deira City Centre

## Bussola

Italian

The Westin Dubai Mina Seyahi
Beach Resort & Marina, Al Sufouh          04 399 4141

A Sicilian influence on the menu means the choices are slightly more adventurous than your standard Italian fare, but all are worth your attention. Save room for dessert because the chef's creations are art on a plate. The open-air first-floor veranda serves cocktails and pizza to a backdrop of sparkling sea views and chill-out tunes. **Map** 2 B1 **Metro** Nakheel

## Café Arabesque

Arabic

Park Hyatt Dubai, Port Saeed

04 602 1234

Whether you choose buffet or a la carte, linger over a cold mezze spread, succulent wood-fired kebabs and fantastic Lebanese, Syrian and Jordanian dishes, as you take in marvellous views of the creek. With romantic, soft lighting, the perfect evening awaits. **Map** 5 C7 **Metro** GGICO

## The Cavendish Restaurant

International

Bonnington Jumeirah Lakes Towers,
  Jumeirah Lakes Towers

04 356 0600

This all-day dining restaurant is a JLT gem: the informal, but sophisticated vibe blends well with its relaxed menu and appropriately attentive staff. Tuck into tasty European dishes such as braised pork belly and butter beans, duck 'bangers', or choose from the odd Arabic and Indian options. The dining area is bright, modern and perfect for family meals or more intimate affairs, and larger groups can book the private dining area. **Map** 2 A2 **Metro** Jumeirah Lakes Towers

## The Cellar

International

The Aviation Club, Al Garhoud

04 282 9333

Diners enjoy their own space in a well-lit room of soaring arches and unexpected stained glass. The outside terrace is also pleasantly relaxed. The a la carte Saturday brunch is recommended. The Cellar's international menu has some favourites and some innovations and the wine list, with special bargains on Saturday and Sunday evenings, shows a surprisingly unusual range. **Map** 5 C8 **Metro** GGICO

## Creekside
Japanese

Sheraton Dubai Creek Hotel & Towers, Deira          04 207 1750

One of the best Japanese restaurants in the city, Creekside now runs 'theme nights' every night of the week. In other words, it has become an all-you-can-eat paradise. The restaurant's clean lines and bright interior make a great setting for large groups, and the food, though limited in variety, far exceeds the buffet norm.  **Map** 5 C4 **Metro** Union

## Counter Culture
Cafe

Dubai Marriott Harbour
  Hotel & Suites, Dubai Marina          04 319 4000

Deli delights lie within this gem, which features relaxing leather chairs, wooden shelves and a contemporary colour scheme. Counter Culture serves up fresh bread baked on the premises (you can watch), daily hot and cold specials, huge salads, chunky sandwiches and homemade icecream. It's licensed and open 24 hours.  **Map** 2 A1 **Metro** Dubai Marina

## The Dhow
Seafood

Le Meridien Mina Seyahi
  Beach Resort & Marina, Al Sufouh          04 399 3333

From the moment you walk down the candlelit path and step aboard this permanently moored dhow you know you're in for a treat. You can choose to dine in the air-conditioned lower deck or go alfresco and enjoy the view of the marina and the ocean from the top deck. The menu focuses heavily on seafood, starting with fresh oysters and a tantalising choice of sushi and sashimi.  **Map** 2 B1 **Metro** Dubai Marina

### Eauzone

Far Eastern
One&Only Royal Mirage, Al Sufouh        04 399 9999

One of the most romantic restaurants in Dubai, Eauzone
has poolside tables, low lighting and sublime exotic food.
The attentive staff, including one of the best sommeliers in
town, are happy to explain dishes. The Asian inspired options
include sushi, scallops, risotto and Thai prawns but, with
curve balls such as foie gras thrown in, you'll find surprises
with every page of the menu.  **Map** 2 B1  **Metro** Nakheel

### El Malecon

Latin American
Dubai Marine Beach Resort & Spa, Jumeira        04 346 1111

El Malecon's high turquoise walls, big windows that overlook
a glowing lagoon and low lighting create a sultry Cuban
atmosphere that builds up slowly during the course of the
evening, helped along by the live music and Salsa dancers.
And while the menu isn't massive (the signature paella is the
best choice), the clientele is undeniably tasty.
**Map** 1 N3  **Metro** Al Jafiliya

### Epicure

Cafe
Desert Palm Dubai, Warsan        04 323 8888

This licensed gourmet deli serves freshly baked bread, fruit
compotes, and a range of cooked breakfasts while you gaze
out over the Desert Palm's swimming pool and polo fields.
A delicious range of lunch dishes and light snacks is also
available. Although a bit out in the sticks – Epicure's offerings
are great for a casual lunch.  **Map** 1 Q11

Fakhreldine

### The Exchange Grill
Steakhouse

Fairmont Dubai, Trade Centre          04 311 8316

The Exchange Grill is the epitome of excess with outsized leather armchairs, modern art installations and a floor-to-ceiling chandelier. The menu strikes balances classicism and innovation, and both lunch and dinner menus offer the best quality beef. **Map** 3 D1 **Metro** World Trade Centre

### Fakhreldine
Arabic/Lebanese

Mövenpick Hotel Bur Dubai, Oud Metha          04 336 6000

From your first dip into the creamy hummus to the last crumb of Arabic sweets, the quality is apparent and the bill isn't too

painful. Choose from rarer Arabic dishes and old favourites as you watch the gyrating belly dancer.

**Map** 5 A6 **Metro** Oud Metha

### Fire & Ice – Raffles Grill
Steakhouse

Raffles Dubai, Umm Hurair                04 314 9888

Once a molecular gastronomy experiment, Fire & Ice has rebranded into an upscale steakhouse, complete with a signature sauce and massive wine list. The service is what you'd expect from a Raffles restaurant and the steaks well prepared. **Map** 5 A7 **Metro** Healthcare City

### The Fish Market
Seafood

Radisson Blu Hotel, Dubai Deira Creek, Al Rigga    04 222 7171

Accompanied by a member of staff clad in plastic gloves and clutching a wicker shopping basket, you can select fresh fish, then request the style of cooking. While you wait for your tailor-made dinner to arrive you can snack on a bowl of french fries and soak up the creekside view.

**Map** 5 C3 **Metro** Union

### Flavours On Two
International

Towers Rotana Hotel, Trade Centre          04 343 8000

This stylish, busy 'dinner brunch' venue focuses on a different global cuisine each night, including British and Italian. The wide range of dishes includes cold starters, hot grills and delicious desserts. Free-flowing alcohol is included in the reasonable cover charge, or you can upgrade to champagne.

**Map** 3 C1 **Metro** Financial Centre

### Glasshouse Brasserie

European

Hilton Dubai Creek, Deira

04 227 1111

Sample a taste of the Mediterranean at this chic brasserie with glass walls, dark woods, tasteful colours, and Mondrian-style paintings. The menu provides contemporary dishes with a touch of flair. It's a good spot for a business lunch or a lively group dinner. A Friday brunch is available with free-flowing drink options, including champagne.

**Map** 5 C4 **Metro** Al Rigga

### Hofbräuhaus

German

JW Marriott Hotel, Deira

04 607 7977

From the sauerkraut to the white sausage with sweet mustard, everything here is authentically Bavarian. Add in the beer hall decor, traditional garb for the staff and accordion music and you have a recipe for a fun night out. Several German beers are on tap, along with a full selection of wines and spirits. **Map** 5 D5 **Metro** Abu Baker Al Siddique

### iZ

Indian

Grand Hyatt Dubai, Umm Hurair

04 317 1234

iZ's dark, contemporary interior is a beautifully designed space, complete with hardwood screens, sculptures and private rooms. The perfectly prepared Indian dishes are presented tapas style, with tandoori items served by the piece – ideal for sampling several flavours. Expect gourmet Indian cuisine that respects tradition.

**Map** 5 A8 **Metro** Healthcare City

### JW's Steakhouse
Steakhouse

JW Marriott Hotel, Deira
04 607 7977

Set in an intimate, secluded part of the hotel, JW's Steakhouse makes its intentions clear the moment you walk through the door when chefs can be seen cleaving huge chunks of meat in the open kitchen. Once you are shown to your stately leather armchair, a huge menu offering an impressive range of steak and seafood awaits.

**Map** 5 D5 **Metro** Abu Baker Al Siddique

### Khazana
Indian

Al Nasr Leisureland, Oud Metha
04 336 0061

Indian celebrity chef Sanjeev Kapoor's spacious, popular eatery specialises in cuisine from northern India. All dishes are well prepared and served in big portions, but the prawn curry and chicken tikka are the most popular. Other delicacies include grilled tandoori seafood, a variety of rice dishes and some hearty gravy-based dishes.

**Map** 5 A6 **Metro** Oud Metha

### Kitsune
Japanese

Fairmont Dubai, Trade Centre
04 332 7660

Every aspect of Kitsune is surreal, from the white leather, polished gold trim and dark red floral decor to the bizarre fog machines and temple chants that periodically sneak up on you. The food is just as thrilling, if a bit less baffling – black cod, wagyu beef and sushi dominate the pricey menu. If you're looking to impress, a reservation at Kitsune will surely do the trick.  **Map** 3 D1 **Metro** World Trade Centre

Glasshouse Brasserie

## La Baie

Seafood

The Ritz-Carlton Dubai, Dubai Marina          04 399 4000

In Dubai's 24 hour hectic culture, it's easy to forget how to luxuriate over a meal. La Baie reminds you. If the music doesn't massage away stress, the wine list showcases some stunning tension relievers. With Korean-Japanese and French chefs at the helm, the resulting food is an exciting mix of traditional and imaginative sushi and seafood.

**Map** 2 A1 **Metro** Dubai Marina

## Latino House

Latin American

Al Murooj Rotana Hotel & Suites, Trade Centre     04 321 1111

Latino House uses heavy drapes, marble decor and dim lighting to intoxicate before the food even appears. Succulent steaks, modernised classics and imaginative new creations make up the small but tempting menu. Submit to the Latin vibe with dancing on Mondays.

**Map** 3 C2 **Metro** Financial Centre

## Levantine

Arabic

Atlantis The Palm, Palm Jumeirah          04 426 2626

This could be Dubai's ultimate upscale Lebanese dining venue. Popular set menus provide a delicious spread of hot and cold mezze, mains and desserts, and an extensive a la carte menu allows the more adventurous to try new dishes. The wine list includes several Lebanese selections, while belly dancing and shisha complete the experience.

**Map** 1 D1 **Metro** Nakheel

La Baie

### The Lime Tree Café
Cafe

Jumeira Rd, Nr Jumeira Mosque, Jumeira    04 349 8498

Set in a converted villa on Jumeira Road, this impressive cafe has become a Dubai institution. The understated interior features trendy plastic chairs, dark wood tables and lime-green washed walls. With a definite nod towards Mediterranean cuisine, there's plenty of paninis filled with wholesome ingredients, as well as delicious couscous salads, satay kebabs and the best carrot cake in the city.

**Map** 1 N1 **Metro** Jafiliya

### The Lobby Lounge
Afternoon Tea

The Ritz-Carlton, Dubai, Dubai Marina    04 399 4000

Tea at the Ritz is an exquisite experience. Delicate finger sandwiches and dainty pastries, succulent scones with clotted cream and a selection of jams, a fabulously colonial selection of teas and the fine china are all deliciously regal. It feels exclusive, but all are welcome. Reservations are recommended.  **Map** 2 A1 **Metro** Dubai Marina

### Magnolia
Vegetarian

Al Qasr Hotel, Umm Suqeim    04 366 6730

Magnolia is Dubai's first fine dining vegetarian restaurant, and its kitchen is skilled enough to impress the most ardent meat eaters. Complimentary appetisers, between-course amuses-bouches and main courses are imaginatively concocted using home-grown vegetables and herbs. There's also a wine list if you need something sinful to counteract the spa cuisine.

**Map** 2 D1 **Metro** Mall of the Emirates

### Mahi Mahi
Wafi, Umm Hurair

Seafood
04 324 4100

Mahi Mahi's options are endless – live mud crab from Africa, feisty langoustines from Norway, fresh red snapper, local helwayoo, hammour and more, all prepared in a choice of delicious sauces from the across the planet. The portions are plentiful and served with panache and organic vegetables in a beautiful setting with welcoming smiles.

**Map** 5 A7 **Metro** Healthcare City

### Majlis Al Bahar
Burj Al Arab, Umm Suqeim

Mediterranean
04 301 7600

Part of the Burj Al Arab, Majlis Al Bahar offers front row seats to the iconic hotel's nightly light show. The meaty Mediterranean cuisine isn't exceptional but the mini barbecues are a novel attraction, and the salads are well executed. Come prepared to spend some dirhams – this one certainly isn't for the cost conscious.

**Map** 2 D1 **Metro** Mall of the Emirates

### Manhattan Grill
Grand Hyatt Dubai, Umm Hurair

Steakhouse
04 317 1234

Compared to the indoor rainforest of the hotel's lobby, Manhattan Grill is the ultimate in low-key chic. Soft lighting, plush seating, smooth music and an excellent selection of succulent steaks make this one of the finest fine-dining venues in town. There are seafood and vegetarian dishes on the menu too. It's on the pricey side, but you certainly get what you pay for here. **Map** 5 A8 **Metro** Healthcare City

## Margaux

European

Souk Al Bahar, Downtown Dubai                         04 439 9755

Although many factors jostle for your attention here, like the view of the Burj Khalifa, the impressive fountains, or the extensive wine list, the food is the undisputed star of the show. French and Italian cuisines mingle successfully on the menu, which includes an ample range of meat, seafood and vegetarian dishes. Make sure you leave enough room for the cheesecake, which is the best in Dubai.

**Map** 3 B2  **Metro** Burj Khalifa/Dubai Mall

## Marina

Seafood

Jumeirah Beach Hotel, Umm Suqeim                      04 406 8999

Located at the end of the pier, Marina serves a selection of seafood cooked largely under Asian influence, but unfortunately, the restaurants' glass obstructs the gorgeous view. The restaurant is open during the evenings from 18:30.

**Map** 2 D1  **Metro** Mall of the Emirates

## The Market Place

International

JW Marriott Hotel, Deira                              04 607 7977

Friendly and welcoming, The Market Place is another of Dubai's top all-you-can-eat restaurants. No sooner have you sat down than the waiter brings what will undoubtedly be the first beverage of many – you won't sit with an empty glass for long. It is the food that distinguishes this buffet restaurant which has with live-cooking stations and a most impressive buffet of starters and desserts.

**Map** 5 D5  **Metro** Abu Baker Al Siddique

## Marrakech
Moroccan

Shangri-La Hotel, Trade Centre
04 343 8888

Smooth arches and lamps add to an overwhelming sense of tranquility, while a duo belts out traditional tunes on Marrakech's small stage. Starters such as wedding pie with pigeon, crushed almonds and icing sugar, are served on blue ceramic. Don't miss the lamb tagine with fluffy, fragrant rice.

**Map** 3 C1 **Metro** Financial Centre

## The Meat Co
Steakhouse

Souk Al Bahar, Downtown Dubai
04 420 0737

This popular South African chain is more than just a string of steakhouses. The well-planned decor matches the thoughtful menu. Start with a mezze appetiser platter, then move on to a healthy lamb skewer with peppers, or an enormous steak with your choice of carbs. Even the burgers feel like fine dining. There is another restaurant at Souk Madinat Jumeirah (04 368 6040), which has alfresco tables by the water.

**Map** 3 B2 **Metro** Burj Khalifa/Dubai Mall

## Méridien Village Terrace
International

Le Meridien Dubai, Al Garhoud
04 702 2449

Only open in winter and beautifully lit at night, this large space manages to feel intimate for couples but is also perfect for larger groups. Each night there is a different culinary theme: Caribbean, Mexican, BBQ or Arabic. Numerous live-cooking stations keep the food wonderfully fresh. The great choice of drinks are replenished with alarming regularity.

**Map** 5 D8 **Metro** GGICO

### Mirai
Souk Al Bahar, Downtown Dubai

Japanese
04 439 7333

Its competition is steep, but Mirai's head chef is creative enough to make it one of the top contemporary Japenese restaurants in the city. Standouts like roasted scallops with foie gras and jalapeno dressing will blow you away, and the tender short ribs will make you weep. Mirai's cocktails and desserts are just as enticing, and the red and black contemporary decor will impress you from the start.

**Map** 3 B2 **Metro** Burj Khalifa/Dubai Mall

### Momotaro
Souk Al Bahar, Downtown Dubai

Japanese
04 425 7976

Rather than choose a solitary main, the friendly staff will rightly encourage you to taste a selection from the menu of tempura, sushi, noodles and soups. The slick interior, a tasteful mix of dark wood, red lighting and white square tables, is a fitting residence for the elegant dishes that quickly arrive at your table.

**Map** 3 B2 **Metro** Burj Khalifa/Dubai Mall

### M's Beef Bistro
Le Meridien Dubai, Al Garhoud

Steakhouse
04 702 2700

M's Beef Bistro is unpretentious with an opulent feel, offering excellent service and cuisine, in the mid-price range. Ideal for a smart lunch or dinner, the wine list is comprehensive and the menu offers excellent steaks and French dishes; look out for le classiques including french onion soup and burgundy snails. **Map** 5 D8 **Metro** GGICO

## Munchi

Far Eastern

Habtoor Grand Resort & Spa, Dubai Marina        04 399 5000

Munchi offers great Thai food and sushi, with excellent service. Dine alfresco on the patio in the green hotel grounds, or inside at this stylish bamboo hut-style restaurant. The sharing starter platter gets the juices flowing, and there's live cooking for the showpiece dishes where the adept staff will helpfully explain which sauces go well with each dish.

**Map** 2 A1  **Metro** Dubai Marina

## Nasimi

International

Atlantis The Palm, Palm Jumeirah        04 426 2626

Nasimi surprises with its simplicity. It offers a small, delectable menu of seafood and meat dishes, all expertly prepared, and one of the best alfresco settings in the city. The large terrace offers views of either the pool or the Palm, perfect for a day of lounging, and the beach-side beanbags turn into a popular place to see and be seen on weekend evenings.

**Map** 1 D1  **Metro** Nakheel

## Nina

Indian

One&Only Royal Mirage, Al Sufouh        04 399 9999

Massive chandeliers and graceful candelabra cast muted light on faux marble walls and tiled circular arches at Nina. Percussive music accompanies conventional Indian main courses flanked by inventive starters and desserts. The staff know the ingredients of each dish and provide diners with time to reflect on the food and the lively atmosphere.

**Map** 2 B1  **Metro** Nakheel

## Nineteen

European

The Address Montgomerie Dubai,
  Emirates Living                                   04 363 1275

The Montgomerie's flagship restaurant serves up rotisserie-style food in chic surrounds and the show kitchen is loud and proud. With views over the hotel's lush grounds, it hosts a popular Friday brunch and a satisfying Saturday roast.
**Map** 2 A3 **Metro** Dubai Marina

## Nobu

Japanese

Atlantis The Palm, Palm Jumeirah           04 426 2626

Nobuyuki Matsuhisa has upped the ante for sushi in the city. Japanese food aficionados will love the exceptional quality, attention to detail and huge menu of sushi, sashimi and tempura. The uninitiated will quickly feel at home thanks to the helpful, friendly staff. Nobu is not restricted to celebrities, and you're always welcome, as long as you can get a reservation. **Map** 1 D1 **Metro** Nakheel

## The Observatory

International

Dubai Marriott Harbour
  Hotel & Suites, Dubai Marina                 04 319 4000

It's all about the view at this atmospheric 52nd floor gastro-lounge. Spectacular 360° vistas over the Marina and The Palm accompany the concise (but tasty) menu, while the cocktails are excellent. Arrive before sunset then stay for the evening to enjoy the panorama in full.
**Map** 2 A1 **Metro** Dubai Marina

## Okku

Japanese

The Monarch Dubai, Trade Centre

04 501 8777

There's more than enough to make you go 'mmm!' at Okku: the trendy dark wood decor, so very low lighting and amazing food. If prices are ever a sign of substance, then it definitely drives the point home, but its menu of sushi, sashimi and tempura is so fancifully executed, on this occasion, you may have to agree. Take the luxury up a notch and book one of the chic tatami rooms for private dining or sip inventive cocktails in the swanky bar. **Map** 3 D1 **Metro** World Trade Centre

## Ossiano

Seafood

Atlantis The Palm, Palm Jumeirah

04 426 2626

Three Michelin star chef Santi Santamaria serves up Catalan-inspired simple, delicate seafood dishes at this impeccable eatery. Glistening chandeliers and floor-to-ceiling views of the enormous Ambassador Lagoon provide a formal, but romantic, setting for guests to enjoy Santamaria's incredible, and incredibly priced, seafood. This is an absolute must if you can afford it. **Map** 1 D1 **Metro** Nakheel

## Pachanga

Latin American

Hilton Dubai Jumeirah Resort, Dubai Marina

04 399 1111

Choose from the Havana-style bar, Brazilian barbecue, Mexican lounge or Argentinean terrace that surround the dancefloor at this hotspot. Start with fresh guacamole prepared at your table, then move onto the wide selection of mains: the seafood is delicious but the real winners are meat-eaters. Wednesday is tango night. **Map** 2 A1 **Metro** Dubai Marina

Okku

### PaiThai

Thai

Al Qasr Hotel, Umm Suqeim                     04 366 8888

You'll have a night to remember at PaiThai, from the abra ride
to the restaurant to the novel Thai cuisine. If you are lucky,
at some point in the evening, you will be entertained by a
traditionally dressed Thai dancer whose precise movements
are as magnificent as the food. The outdoor seating area
provides delightful views in the winter months and the menu
provides the odd twist on familiar favourites.

**Map** 2 D1 **Metro** Mall of the Emirates

### Pars Iranian Kitchen

Persian

Nr Rydges Plaza, Al Satwa                     04 398 4000

Pars offers a traditional laid-back atmosphere a million miles
from the modernity suggested by its neon sign. The menu
is limited, but includes staples such as hummus, moutabel,
tabbouleh, and a selection of grilled meats, kebabs and
Iranian stews. Its delightful front garden, enclosed by a fairy
light-entwined hedgerow, is home to low tables and soft,
majlis bench seats, perfect for enjoying a leisurely shisha with
a group of friends. **Map** 1 N4 **Metro** Al Jafiliya

### Peppercrab

Singaporean

Grand Hyatt Dubai, Umm Hurair                 04 317 1234

One of Dubai's best Asian restaurants, Peppercrab serves
noodles and chilli crab so authentic you'll feel like you're
sitting in the middle of Newton's Circus in Singapore. Service
is exceptional and the price, while on the high side, is worth it
for this classy venue. **Map** 5 A8 **Metro** Healthcare City

## Persia Persia

Persian

Pharaohs' Club, Wafi, Umm Hurair
04 324 4100

Located at the top of the Wafi Pyramids, Persia Persia's interior is simple yet elegant. Choose from flavour-packed appetisers that are great for sharing, alongside regional favourites such as kebabs and lamb stew. The fact that it's a regular hangout for many Iranians reflects its quality.

**Map** 5 A7 **Metro** Healthcare City

## Pierchic

Seafood

Al Qasr Hotel, Umm Suqeim
04 366 8888

Pierchic has the best location of any Dubai restaurant. Perched at the end of a long wooden pier that juts into the Arabian Gulf, it affords front-row seats of an unobstructed Burj Al Arab, as well as Dubai Marina and Palm Jumeriah in the distance. The delicately presented seafood and famed wine list come at a price but what you're really paying for is the view, especially if you request a table on the terrace.

**Map** 2 D1 **Metro** Mall of the Emirates

## Pisces

Seafood

Souk Madinat Jumeirah, Umm Suqeim
04 366 6730

Flawless in every sense, Pisces could be the perfect seafood restaurant. Professional service, delicious, artistically presented food and beautifully set, intimate tables all score full points. The winning detail is the outdoor bar with a breathtaking view of the Madinat waterways.

**Map** 2 D1 **Metro** Mall of the Emirates

Going Out

Restaurants & Cafes

### Rare Restaurant

Steakhouse

Desert Palm Dubai, Warsan • 04 323 8888

Although it isn't cheap, Rare's menu has enough selection to please both the serious carnivore and the picky gourmand. In the cooler months, book a table outside on the gorgeously contemporary terrace overlooking the polo fields to take advantage of the hotel's isolated setting. A good pick for a romantic tete-a-tete. **Map** 1 Q11

### Ravi's

Pakistani

Al Satwa Rd, Nr Satwa R/A, Al Satwa • 04 331 5353

This much-loved diner offers a range of Pakistani curried favourites, rice dishes and freshly baked naan, alongside more adventurous fare such as fried brains. The venue is basic, with most people opting to sit outside with all of Satwa life on show, but the food excels and you can eat like a king for under Dhs.30. Dining is also available in the main restaurant or in the quieter family section. **Map** 1 N4 **Metro** Al Jafiliya

### Reem Al Bawadi

Arabic/Lebanese

Jumeira Rd, Nr HSBC, Jumeira • 04 394 7444

Semi-isolated booths with thick Arabic cushions line the walls, while tables lined with armchairs fill the dark, bustling dining area. Reem Al Bawadi's mostly-Arab clientele is a good sign that the grills and mezze coming out of its kitchen are authentic. Best of all, the place is designed for post-meal relaxation with shisha and tea in hand.
**Map** 1 L3 **Metro** Burj Khalifa/Dubai Mall

## The Rib Room

Steakhouse

Emirates Towers Hotel, Trade Centre          04 319 8088

The deep red upholstery and dark woods create an elegant contemporary Asian feel at The Rib Room. The well-rounded menu has a host of hot and cold starters, numerous steaks and an array of seafood but, bizarrely, no ribs. Excellent service, a warm intimate atmosphere and delicious food make for a satisfying Sheikh Zayed Road experience.

**Map** 3 D2  **Metro** Emirates Towers

## Ronda Locatelli

Italian

Atlantis The Palm, Palm Jumeirah          04 426 2626

The cavernous interior seats hundreds in raised alcoves or at tables surrounding the centrepiece of the restaurant, a huge stone-built wood-fired pizza oven. The casual menu offers a large selection of starters, pasta and mains, as well as a range of small dishes for sharing. Prices are quite reasonable for such a connected restaurant.  **Map** 1 D1  **Metro** Nakheel

## Rostang

French

Atlantis The Palm, Palm Jumeirah          04 426 2626

Rostang's wood trim, leather bench seating and dim lighting perfectly mimic the decor of a French bistro from the 1930s. The food is just as reminiscent. Two-star Michelin chef Michel Rostang's seafood-heavy menu is hardly simple, but full of comforting dishes that shy away from experimentation and concentrate on preparation and presentation.

**Map** 1 D1  **Metro** Nakheel

### Sahn Eddar

Afternoon Tea

Burj Al Arab, Umm Suqeim

04 301 7600

Those with normal-sized pockets won't get a better opportunity to inspect the Burj Al Arab. This is where you can slurp tea and nibble expensive scones at the base of the world's tallest atrium. There's an endless feast of delicious sandwiches, scones, cakes, sweets and a pot of your choice of the finest teas. After, consider a drink at the Skyview Bar for the stunning vistas 200m above the sea.

**Map** 2 D1  **Metro** Mall of the Emirates

### Salmontini

Seafood

Mall of the Emirates, Al Barsha

04 341 0222

Salmontini's chic interior is fashioned around large windows overlooking the mall's indoor ski slope. Choose from a selection of Scottish salmon, worked in every possible way (from smoked and grilled to cured and poached). All-inclusive deals offered during the week make a night here more cost-effective.  **Map** 2 D3  **Metro** Mall of the Emirates

### Saravana Bhavan

Indian

Karama Park Square, Al Karama

04 334 5252

Taking its name from the much-loved hotel Saravana Bhavan in Chennai, India, this unassuming joint is arguably the best of the area's south Indian restaurants. The menu is long enough to keep Indian expatriates interested but it's the thalis that draw crowds. For around Dhs.10 you can get a plate packed with colour and flavours, dal and chapatti. Fine Indian food doesn't come much cheaper.  **Map** 5 A5  **Metro** Al Karama

## Seafire

Atlantis The Palm, Palm Jumeirah

Steakhouse
04 426 2626

The warm colours at Seafire contrast nicely with the rest of Atlantis, while the smell of leather and cosy alcoves conspire to create the vibe of something well-established. Seafood and steak dominate the menu; all of it expertly prepared, and the signature dessert, a trio of chocolate treats, is worth waiting for. **Map** 1 D1 **Metro** Nakheel

## Segreto

Dar Al Masyaf, Souk Madinat Jumeirah, Umm Suqeim

Italian

04 366 6730

Segreto is tucked away, but once inside, its smooth lines, pristine presentation, and warm sandy tones give it a contemporary spin. Your dining journey can begin with sweet champagne cocktails and delicious breads. The food is aesthetically appealing, if a little lacking in consistency, while portions are more suited to a catwalk model than a prop forward. **Map** 2 D1 **Metro** Mall of the Emirates

## Shahrzad

Hyatt Regency Hotel, Deira

Persian
04 209 1234

Shahrzad's interior seems a bit dated, but the live Persian music and copper-clad open kitchen give it an exciting atmosphere. Start with the interesting ash irishta noodle soup, then move on to the equally tasty appetiser platter before digging in to some of the best kebabs in town. **Map** 5 D2 **Metro** Palm Deira

### Shang Palace
Chinese

Shangri-La Hotel, Trade Centre 04 405 2703

Shang Palace's food is delicious and the attentive staff are available to guide newcomers through the numerous options. Familiar dishes are well prepared, and set menus are available. With shark fin soup, live seafood, dim sum and then some, this is certainly a place for something different. A well-stocked bar makes this a suitable venue to start an evening, or round one off. **Map** 3 C1 **Metro** Financial Centre

### Shoo Fee Ma Fee
Moroccan

Souk Madinat Jumeirah, Umm Suqeim 04 366 6730

This is perhaps the only place in Dubai where you can choose between traditional Moroccan dishes of lamb, chicken, goat and camel. After eating your fill, head to the terrace for pastries, shisha, live entertainment and a mesmerising postcard-perfect vista.
**Map** 2 D1 **Metro** Mall of the Emirates

### Spectrum On One
International

Fairmont Dubai, Trade Centre 04 332 5555

With probably the most diverse menu in Dubai, Spectrum on One caters for a variety of tastes throughout each course. The menu takes at least a half hour to read and features both adventurous and familiar dishes from southern Asia, coastal Thailand, Japan, India and Europe. Taste them all in a few hours at the fabulous champagne brunch on Fridays.
**Map** 3 D1 **Metro** World Trade Centre

Spectrum on One

## Spice Island
International

Renaissance Dubai Hotel, Deira
04 262 5555

When it comes to choice, it doesn't come much wider than Spice Island. Diners of every taste, from Italian to Mongolian, will be satisfied by the mouthwateringly varied buffet. The Friday and Saturday brunches are also hugely popular with families (it is smoke-free and includes a kid's area with balloons and face painting) and those looking for some hangover grease. **Map** 5 D4 **Metro** Salahuddin

## Splendido
Italian

The Ritz-Carlton, Dubai, Dubai Marina
04 399 4000

Head to Splendido for a large menu (literally) featuring some excellent, classic Italian fare. Tasty mains and delicious desserts are all generously portioned, and the tone is quietly

classy. There's a good wine list too. A great location for a stroll along the beach afterwards. **Map** 2 A1 **Metro** Dubai Marina

### Sumibiya
Korean

Radisson Blu Hotel Dubai
Deira Creek, Al Rigga                                                 04 222 7171

Eating is a social affair at this yakiniku (Korean grilled meat) eatery, where diners entertain themselves using the gas grill in the middle of every table to sear, grill and charcoal bite-size morsels. It's informal, fun and tasty; if your food is overdone, you only have yourself to blame. **Map** 5 C3 **Metro** Union

### Sushi Sushi
Japanese

Century Village, Al Garhoud                                        04 282 9908

Offering a very comprehensive menu of sushi and sashimi, non-sushi eaters are equally well catered for with alternative Japanese dishes. Tuesday nights see an all you can eat offer for Dhs.169. Reservations are recommended, especially on Tuesdays. **Map** 5 C8 **Metro** GGICO

### Tagine
Moroccan

One&Only Royal Mirage, Al Sufouh                                  04 399 9999

Beneath ground level, through an enormous wooden door, past a majlis area draped in rich embroidery and perfumed with incense you'll find the authentic Tagine. The low-seating and traditionally dressed waiters create a traditional vibe, even if the pastillas, aromatic tagines, spicy kebabs and exotic couscous don't live up to their billing.
**Map** 2 B1 **Metro** Nakheel

### Teatro
International

Towers Rotana Hotel, Trade Centre     04 343 8000

For awesome views of Sheikh Zayed Road served up with fantastic food head to Teatro. The creative menus will please most diners, with standard Japanese fare alongside palate pleasers such as fresh pasta with lobster. Trendy design features and an impressive glass wine cellar complete the experience. **Map** 3 C1 **Metro** Financial Centre

### The Terrace
International

Park Hyatt Dubai, Port Saeed     04 602 1234

Sweep through the Park Hyatt's greenery and you'll reach The Terrace. Awash with icy, contemporary white, chrome and wood, the space-age interior extends out through shiny conservatory doors to an awning-adorned terrace. Scattered with couches and wooden tables, this gorgeous alfresco spot gazes out over the yachts and the multi-lit creek beyond. **Map** 5 C7 **Metro** GGICO

### The Thai Kitchen
Thai

Park Hyatt Dubai, Port Saeed     04 602 1234

Intertwined around four live-cooking areas where all the ingredients are displayed and prepared, Thai Kitchen is a slick, contemporary dining space. With small, tapas-style portions at reasonable prices, your best bet is to order two or three per person and share. The duck curry is outstanding and the attentive staff will keep the sticky rice coming. **Map** 5 C7 **Metro** GGICO

### Thiptara

Seafood

The Palace – The Old Town,
  Downtown Dubai

04 428 7961

Expect fresh and spicy seafood at this quality Thai restaurant overlooking the Burj Khalifa and lake. There's a lively lobster tank from which to take your pick, while the wine list is extensive. This is a hard location to beat for impressing visitors and business associates.

**Map** 3 B2 **Metro** Burj Khalifa/Dubai Mall

### tokyo@thetowers

Japanese

Boulevard at Emirates Towers, Trade Centre

04 319 8088

With elegantly partitioned tatami rooms, lively teppanyaki tables and an eclectic menu, tokyo@thetowers offers diners enough options to keep things interesting. The private rooms all have traditional floor cushions and you can dine by the windows overlooking the mall if you need a view.

**Map** 3 D2 **Metro** Emirates Towers

### Trader Vic's

Polynesian

Souk Madinat Jumeirah, Al Sufouh

04 366 5646

Until you've experienced Trader Vic's, you can't consider yourself a seasoned night-lifer. Delicious Asian-inspired dishes and moreish snacks are available or you can jump straight to the famously exotic cocktails, served in ceramic skulls and seashells. Head to the Crowne Plaza branch (04 331 1111) for live Cuban music every night.

**Map** 2 D1 **Metro** Mall of the Emirates

GOVERNMENT OF DUBAI

DUBAI MUNICIPALITY

# Make your family and friends

## smile

Live Dolphin & Seal Shows

Swimming with Dolphins

**FOR RESERVATIONS**
Call: +971 4 336 9773, Fax: +971 4 336 9774
Email: info@dubaidolphinarium.ae
Location: Umm Hurair 2, Creek Park, Gate 1, Dubai
Online Booking: www.dubaidolphinarium.ae

**Toll Free: 800-DOLPHIN (3657446)**

DUBAI
DOLPHINARIUM

Our Vision: To create an excellent city that provides the essence of success and comfort of living.

### Traiteur
European

Park Hyatt Dubai, Port Saeed
04 602 1234

Having descended from an intimate bar via a dramatic staircase, you'll be struck by the restaurant's soaring ceilings. Traiteur's beautiful open kitchen then provides a great focal point for the French and modern European cuisine. The menu is ordered by ingredient, a flourish typical of this showy restaurant. Head to The Terrace (p.281) afterwards.

**Map** 5 C7 **Metro** GGICO

### Troyka
Russian

Ascot Hotel, Bur Dubai
04 352 0900

Troyka's old world charm creates an intimate mood to enjoy tasty cuisine in. The Tuesday night buffet is all-inclusive and comprises time-honoured delicacies from Russian cuisine. If all you need is a dose of bizarre entertainment, a band plays every night from 22:30 and an extravagant live Vegas-style cabaret begins soon after. **Map** 5 A2 **Metro** Al Fahidi

### Verre By Gordon Ramsay
French

Hilton Dubai Creek, Deira
04 227 1111

You enter through sleek, sliding glass doors, but your first impressions of the decor – understated dark wood furniture and simple white table linen – may leave you wondering what all the fuss is about. However, Gordon Ramsay is a chef, not an interior designer, and Verre is all about the food. Faultless service and the delightful canapes and between-course treats make this a truly memorable dining experience, albeit an expensive one. **Map** 5 C4 **Metro** Al Rigga

## Villa Beach

Mediterranean

Jumeirah Beach Hotel, Umm Suqeim      04 406 8999

The buggy ride to the restaurant's door reveals the killer attraction: you're a bun's throw from the ocean and the Burj Al Arab. The beach-hut aesthetic has a Polynesian vibe but the food is mostly modern Mediterranean. The service is excellent, and although the scenery doesn't come cheap, the food is beautifully prepared and the wine list has been put together with care. **Map** 2 D1 **Metro** Mall of the Emirates

## Vivaldi

Italian

Sheraton Dubai Creek Hotel & Towers, Deira      04 228 1111

Perched over the sparkling Dubai Creek, Vivaldi is a clear contender for the most romantic restaurant in Dubai. Spectacular views from both inside and out on the two terraces, an experimental Italian menu and a comprehensive wine list will have you coming back to try all the delicious selections on offer. **Map** 5 C4 **Metro** Union

## Vu's

Mediterranean

Emirates Towers Hotel, Trade Centre      04 319 8088

A stylish and elegant eatery, this is fine dining at its best and with one of the most sensational views in town. The menu is finely compiled with dishes certain to impress: you can start with caviar linguine and move on to the signature dishes lobster or roast pigeon. Each plate is exquisitely presented and it's often worth a trip for the cocktails alone. Be warned, the location and quality might be sky high but so are the prices. **Map** 3 D2 **Metro** Emirates Towers

# Bars, Pubs & Clubs

Sky-high cocktail lounges, beachside bars, and enough clubs to keep you dancing for a year, all jostle for your evening attention.

### 360°
Bar

Jumeirah Beach Hotel, Umm Suqeim · 04 406 8769

One visit to this Umm Suqeim hottie will leave you smacking your lips with joy – for this is what holidays were made for. Like a static carousel for grown-ups, 360° is a circular rooftop with a bar at its heart. The place boasts stunning panoramic views of the Arabian Gulf. Early arrivals (it opens at 16:00) can take their pick of low white couches and suck whichever colourful shisha they fancy. Sunset signals cocktails, beats and one of the city's best alfreso nights.

**Map** 2 D1  **Metro** Mall of the Emirates

### The Agency
Bar

Souk Madinat Jumeirah, Al Sufouh · 04 366 6730

With a veritable vineyard of the squashed grape on offer, even wine connoisseurs won't fail to find something quaffable on the 30 page wine menu. Dark wood, exposed brickwork and perch-friendly seating complete the chic setting. Tasty tapas-style bites include spring rolls, spicy prawns and delicious olives. There's another branch in Emirates Towers which has a more extensive food menu.

**Map** 2 D1  **Metro** Mall of the Emirates

360°

## Alpha

Nightclub

Le Meridien Dubai, Al Garhoud
04 702 2640

Alpha's high, white interior was formerly a Greek restaurant and its design elements still prevail. A packed schedule of international DJs, special events and drink deals attract a hip, low-key crowd. By spinning some of the best house and hip-hop in Dubai, Alpha raises the musical bar.

**Map** 5 D8 **Metro** GGICO

## The Apartment Lounge + Club

Nightclub

Jumeirah Beach Hotel, Umm Suqeim
04 406 8000

Look out, another champagne cork is popping and yet more photos are being taken for local society mags. Yes, you have

arrived at The Apartment, home to a few high rollers and many beautiful people. The sound system is powerful enough to keep you out of your seat, and the drinks never stop flowing. This is the place for hip-hop and house, all served with lashings of bubbles.

**Map** 2 D1  **Metro** Mall of the Emirates

### Bahri Bar
Bar

Mina A'Salam, Umm Suqeim                               04 366 6730

Imagine you had the chance to design the perfect bar. For starters you'd include a stunning view, with windtower rooftops, rustling palm trees, meandering canals, the towering Burj Al Arab and sparkling ocean beyond. The bar could have rich furnishings, comfortable seating, and ornately engraved lanterns. On the menu you'd make sure a comprehensive cocktail selection was accompanied by wines, beers, and delicious nibbles. Welcome to Bahri Bar.

**Map** 2 D1  **Metro** Mall of the Emirates

### Bar 44
Bar

Grosvenor House, Dubai Marina                          04 399 8888

At Bar 44 waiters with waistcoats that match the bar's carpets whizz around with expensive bottles of champagne, a jazz singer swoons impressively at a grand piano, and plumes of (pricey) cigar smoke fills the air. The cocktails are equally regal. It's best to get here early, say 18:00, when the killer view of luxurious yachts snaking through the marina from the 44th floor can be best enjoyed.

**Map** 2 A1  **Metro** Dubai Marina

## Bar Zar

Bar

Souk Madinat Jumeirah, Al Sufouh          04 366 6730

The upper level of this slick two-floor bar is open in the
middle so you can peer over at the band and drinkers below.
The faux brick walls, art-house prints, small terrace and
laid-back sofas make for a relaxed urban feel. The drinks are
equally eclectic: with beer cocktails (champagne or Smirnoff
Ice with Guinness) and traditional, yet potent, long drinks. Bar
snacks include crab cakes and spring rolls.

**Map** 2 D1  **Metro** Mall of the Emirates

## Barasti

Bar

Le Meridien Mina Seyahi
Beach Resort & Marina, Al Sufouh          04 399 3333

Barasti has beachside beds, a downstairs bar and big screens
for the all-important big games, along with heaps of casual
charm. This laid-back bar is a big expat favourite, loved for
its meaty menu, jugs of Pimms and panoramic vistas, not to
mention the fact you can turn up in flip-flops or Friday finery
depending on your mood.  **Map** 2 B1  **Metro** Dubai Marina

## Belgian Beer Café

Pub

Crowne Plaza Festival City, Festival City          04 701 2222

Aside from the namesake beverage, the main draw are the
moules frites, mussels served in your choice of sauce with
crisp fries and lots of bread for mopping up the juices. The
beer selection is top notch, if expensive. The traditional
dining room fills up fast, as does the gorgeous terrace and the
views are second to none.  **Map** 1 Q7  **Metro** Emirates

### BidiBondi
Bar

Clubhouse Al Manhal,
 Shoreline Apartments, Palm Jumeirah          04 427 0515

This laid-back offering on Palm Jumeirah offers both
indoor and alfresco space, with a beach diner feel nicely
complemented by poolside tables. The menu offers hefty
burgers, sandwiches and salads plus bar snacks, breakfast
and kids' specials. There is also a great range of mocktails,
cocktails, beers and wines. More a spot for a weekend lunch
than romantic liaison, BidiBondi is as relaxed as it gets.
**Map** 1 D1 **Metro** Nakheel

### Blue Bar
Bar

Novotel World Trade Centre, Trade Centre          04 332 0000

Jazz fans unite for some of the best live music in town.
Hidden at the back of the Novotel, the Blue Bar has a relaxed,
low-key vibe with enough 'it' factor to give it cred but without
any delusions of grandeur. You can opt to either pull up a
stool at the large square bar, or get cosy on one of the leather
sofas and armchairs.  **Map** 3 D2 **Metro** World Trade Centre

### Boudoir
Nightclub

Dubai Marine Beach Resort & Spa, Jumeira          04 345 5995

This exclusive spot can be as difficult to get into as a lady's
chamber but once you get past the doormen – as long as
you are appropriately dressed – you will be treated to a
Parisian-style club that's perfect for dangero On the 26th floor
us liaisons. The regular free drinks for ladies help pack the
circular dance floor.  **Map** 1 N3 **Metro** Al Jafiliya

Clockwise from top left: Bar Zar, Vu's, Left Bank

### Buddha Bar

Nightclub

Grosvenor House, Dubai Marina          04 399 8888

Buddha Bar has the wow factor. From the entrance, a seductively lit corridor leads you past private lounges and tucked-away alcoves, all perfectly decadent places to dine, lounge, and socialise. With the Buddha Bar's famous mix of music, some of the best cocktails in town, and a selection of tasty Asian treats, this is a firm favourite among Dubai's army of socialites. **Map** 2 A1 **Metro** Dubai Marina

### Caramel Restaurant & Lounge

Bar

Dubai International Financial Centre, Trade Centre  04 425 6677

This is a place where those who work hard, come to play even harder. Oozing urban cool, the stylish restaurant spills out from the bar through open walls on to the terrace, where cabanas and warm lighting set the mood for stylish lounging. From the Mac n Cheese to the lobster tacos, expect high quality ingredients served with American flair. As you might expect, prices are high. **Map** 3 C2 **Metro** Financial Centre

### Chi@The Lodge

Nightclub

Al Nasr Leisureland, Oud Metha          04 337 9470

The Lodge is always busy with its indoor and outdoor dancefloors, lots of seating and large screens and VIP 'cabanas'. The regular theme nights with fancy dress are popular, especially the legendary 'cheese'. On top of all that, it's easy to get taxis outside, there's often a shawarma stand in the carpark and entrance is free before 22:20 on most nights. **Map** 5 A6 **Metro** Oud Metha

### Cin Cin

Bar

Fairmont Dubai, Trade Centre    04 311 8316

Thick carpet, fat cigars and a hefty wine list await at this city centre spot. It may give the credit card a bashing, but if you are into wine then it is money well spent. The cocktails aren't half-bad, either. The slick bar fills up fast with an upmarket post-work crowd. Light up, sit back and contemplate your fortune. **Map** 3 D1 **Metro** World Trade Centre

### Dhow & Anchor

Pub

Jumeirah Beach Hotel, Umm Suqeim    04 406 8999

Dhow & Anchor's bar is a popular spot, particularly during happy hour and sporting events – try the outdoor terrace if you are dining and enjoy glimpses of the Burj Al Arab. The menu includes the usual range of drinks and terrific curries, roast dinners, pies, and fish and chips.
**Map** 2 D1 **Metro** Mall of the Emirates

### Double Decker

Pub

Al Murooj Rotana Hotel & Suites, Trade Centre    04 321 1111

On a Friday afternoon this could be your average pub in any town. Whether this is good or bad is up to you. With big screen sports, dangerously long happy hours and karaoke, many appreciate the relative charms this pub provides. Fridays are the most crowded thanks to the inexpensive boozy brunch. Somewhat refreshingly, there is little need to worry about dress code; trainers, flip-flops and shorts are all fine. **Map** 3 C2 **Metro** Financial Centre

### Eclipse Bar
Bar

InterContinental Dubai Festival City,
 Festival City 04 701 1111

On the 26th floor, Eclipse is all about glamour, with red leather padded walls, marble tables and a huge bar serving hundreds of different cocktails. A cigar humidor, premium liquors and elegant little canapés strive to make this a first choice for Dubai's hip crowd. It's also a great vantage point for cityscape views of Sheikh Zayed Road's highrises.
**Map** 5 A7 **Metro** Healthcare City

### Healey's Bar & Terrace
Bar

Bonnington Jumeirah Lakes Towers,
 Jumeirah Lakes Towers 04 356 0600

Wednesday nights is the night at Healeys, which has a live dj and three, free drinks for women from 07:30 to 23:00. The stylish bar, with an ultra-chic glass bar, is perfect for glam patrons looking for a place to start the evening. Prop up at the bar and you can almost believe you are sipping cocktails in a Manhattan bar, and not in the middle of Jumeriah Lakes Towers. To top of the drama, head to the terrace, where you can sip cocktails outside surrounded by twinkling marina vistas. **Map** 2 A2 **Metro** Jumeirah Lakes Towers

### Hive
Bar

Souk Al Bahar, Downtown Dubai 04 425 2296

Balearic beats from the resident DJ keep the stylish crowd mingling and tippling until the small hours. The food, a range of pizzas, sushi and Asian dishes, is all exquisitely presented

and the mini burgers taste even better than they look. The vibe of the popular lounge terrace makes up for the pricey drinks. **Map** 3 B2 **Metro** Burj Khalifa/Dubai Mall

### Irish Village
Pub

The Aviation Club, Al Garhoud                                   04 282 4750

The Irish Village is the nearest thing Dubai has to a beer garden, and the best place to go for fish and chips (complete with Guinness batter) and a pint of the dark stuff. Despite being one of the largest pubs in the city, it's almost always packed with people looking for a bit of nostalgia. Expect hearty pub food, twinkling lights in the trees and the odd live musician strumming some Ronan Keating. **Map** 5 C8 **Metro** GGICO

### Jambase
Nightclub

Souk Madinat Jumeirah, Al Sufouh                               04 366 6730

Jambase's tempting selection of cocktails is enough to kick off a good night. There is an authentic 50s style jazz bar atmosphere created by the dark wooden interior and a live band kicking out the jams. The vaguely art deco stylings play host to completely contrasting evenings. Despite serving delicious food, it's best to arrive after 23:00 when the dancefloor fills up. **Map** 2 D1 **Metro** Mall of the Emirates

### Left Bank
Bar

Souk Madinat Jumeirah, Al Sufouh                               04 368 6171

While Left Bank's terrace allows romancing couples a peaceful retreat, the contemporary interior decor welcomes large groups with good tunes and a fine selection of drinks. The bar menu is made up of simple meat and fish dishes – the coriander burger is recommended – along with a selection of nibbles and plates to share. There is also a branch in Souk Al Bahar (04 368 4501).  Map 2 D1  Metro Mall of the Emirates

### Neos                                                          Bar
The Address Downtown Dubai, Downtown Dubai   04 436 8888
Take the elevators to the 63rd floor and be amazed. With huge wall to wall windows, Neos' staggering height makes it impossible to play it cool as you stare out at Burj Khalifa and the city beyond. Such a setting deserves an impressive drinks list and Neos doesn't disappoint.
**Map** 3 B3 **Metro** Burj Khalifa/Dubai Mall

### Nezesaussi                                                    Bar
Al Manzil Hotel, Downtown Dubai                04 428 5888
This upmarket sports bar, home to the best ribs in town, has enough glam to keep women happy while the match is on. Tastefully decked out in memorabilia, Nezesaussi might be a tongue-twister but once you've been, the name is hard to forget. Although it boasts South African sausages, lamb from New Zealand and Australian steaks, it's not all beer and beef.
**Map** 3 B3 **Metro** Burj Khalifa/Dubai Mall

### Oeno Wine Bar                                                 Bar
The Westin Dubai Mina Seyahi
 Beach Resort & Marina, Al Sufouh          04 399 4141
Oeno's decor is modern and stylish, and the wine wall, complete with a librarian-style bookshelf ladder, adds a

sense of decadence. There's a temperature-controlled cheese room with over 50 types of cheese, as well as a menu full of antipasti options. For an unbeatable date, book a table on the terrace.  **Map** 2 B1  **Metro** Nakheel

### Rooftop Lounge & Terrace
Bar
One&Only Royal Mirage, Al Sufouh                04 399 9999
Clever design and lighting combine with a subtle DJ to make this one of Dubai's finest bars. Rooftop has a superb view of Palm Jumeirah, Moroccan decor with comfy majlis-style seating, intimate booths with huge cushions and a good menu of cocktails and bottled beers. If you're looking to kick back and relax under the stars there's no better place.
**Map** 2 B1  **Metro** Nakheel

### Sanctuary
Nightclub
Atlantis The Palm, Palm Jumeirah                04 426 2626
Expect something special from Atlantis; like a suspended catwalk in a nightclub – because that's what you get at Sanctuary, along with lashings of cool. This space is modern, glam and packed with hotel guests and dedicated clubbers. It's open every night of the week but Fridays are when it kicks off with a blend of house, R&B and Arabic music. The outdoor terrace fills up early.  **Map** 1 D1  **Metro** Nakheel

### Sho Cho
Bar
Dubai Marine Beach Resort & Spa, Jumeira                04 346 1111
Sho Cho is a perfectly fine Japanese restaurant but that's not the real reason the beautiful set flock to its shoreline location.

Sho Cho

The sizeable bar, flanked by two alfresco eating areas and guarded by sharp-eyed waiters, is the real attraction. The tiny dancefloor is a poser's paradise; there's barely room to swing a man in tight jeans. **Map** 1 N3 **Metro** Al Jafiliya

### Skyview Bar
Bar

Burj Al Arab, Umm Suqeim                                  04 301 7600

Come here in the evening for high-class cocktails and stunning views. Alternately, come for the afternoon tea and sit back and savour the view while a waiter piles vast quantities of finger sandwiches, mini buns, cakes and biscuits on to your table, accompanied by a pot of tea and a glass of champagne. Book well in advance.

**Map** 2 D1 **Metro** Mall of the Emirates

### Trader Vic's Mai-Tai Lounge
Bar

Oasis Beach Tower, Dubai Marina                          04 399 8993

The livelier cousin of the Crowne Plaza and Madinat Jumeirah eateries, this large bar is decked out in Polynesian style. Mai-Tai's totally tropical cocktail list is accompanied by tasty, if expensive, bar snacks and the spacious dancefloor provides a clubby feel. **Map** 2 A1 **Metro** Dubai Marina

### Uptown Bar
Bar

Jumeirah Beach Hotel, Umm Suqeim                         04 406 8999

Take the elevator to the 24th floor to find this small but perfectly formed bar. The cool interior is classy enough, but Uptown's selling point is the outdoor terrace: it's a perfect spot for 'sunset behind the Burj' photo ops. Get there at 18:00 to take advantage of the half-price happy hour and cute little canapes. The menu features some mouthwatering mocktails and a selection of tasty bar snacks.

**Map** 2 D1 **Metro** Mall of the Emirates

## Warehouse
Bar
Le Meridien Dubai, Al Garhoud
04 702 2560

Warehouse's ground floor contains both an impressively stocked beer bar and well-rounded wine bar. Up the spiral staircase is a dual-personality restaurant – half fine dining and half sushi – where the food is elegantly displayed and deliciously inventive. As if that weren't enough, there's a vodka bar and a lounge club with an intimate dancefloor, DJ booth and just enough flash to warrant dressing up. Both classy and lively, this buzzing spot that is best reserved for big nights out, rather than intimate meetings.

**Map** 5 D8 **Metro** GGICO

## Zinc
Nightclub
Crowne Plaza, Trade Centre
04 331 1111

If it's good enough for Carl Cox, it's probably good enough for you. House fans flock to this slick hotspot, known for its packed dancefloor and cabin crew clientele. With coloured lightboxes, lots of seating and international DJs, any night at Zinc feels like a party night. The hotel is also home to the cosy Oscar's Vine Society.

**Map** 3 D1 **Metro** Emirates Towers

# Index

**Index**

## Live Work Explore Guides

All you need to know about living, working and enjoying
life in these exciting destinations

# Mini Visitors' Guides

Perfect pocket-sized visitors' guides

# Activity Guides

Drive, trek, dive and swim... life will never
be boring again

# Explorer Products

## Mini Maps

Fit the city in your pocket

## Maps

Never get lost again

# Photography Books

Beautiful cities caught through the lens

# Practical & Lifestyle Products & Calendars

The perfect accessories for a buzzing lifestyle

## Explorer Team
Check out www.explorerpublishing.com

### Publishing
**Founder & CEO** Alistair MacKenzie
**Associate Publisher** Claire England

### Editorial
**Editors** Matt Warnock,
Pamela Afram,
Siobhan Campbell
**Corporate Editor** Charlie Scott
**Production Coordinator**
Kathryn Calderon
**Senior Editorial Assistant**
Mimi Stankova
**Editorial Assistant** Ingrid Cupido,
Amapola Castillo

### Design
**Creative Director** Pete Maloney
**Art Director** Ieyad Charaf
**Account Manager** Chris Goldstraw
**Designer** Michael Estrada
**Junior Designer** Didith Hapiz
**Layout Manager** Jayde Fernandes
**Layout Designers** Mansoor Ahmed,
Shawn Zuzarte
**Cartography Manager**
Zainudheen Madathil
**Cartographers** Noushad Madathil,
Sunita Lakhiani
**Traffic Manager** Maricar Ong

### Sales & Marketing
**Group Media Sales Manager**
Peter Saxby
**Media Sales Area Managers**
Laura Zuffa, Lisa Shaver, Pouneh Hafizi
**Media Sales Executive** Bryan Anes

**Marketing & PR Manager**
Annabel Clough
**Marketing & PR Assistant**
Shedan Ebona
**Group Retail Sales Manager**
Ivan Rodrigues
**Senior Retail Sales Merchandisers**
Ahmed Mainodin, Firos Khan
**Retail Sales Merchandisers**
Johny Mathew, Shan Kumar
**Retail Sales Coordinator**
Michelle Mascarenhas
**Retail Sales Drivers** Shabsir Madathil,
Najumudeen K.I.
**Warehouse Assistant** Mohamed Haji

### Photography
**Photography Manager** Pamela Grist
**Photographer** Victor Romero
**Image Editor** Henry Hilos

### Finance & Administration
**Administration Manager**
Shyrell Tamayo
**Accountant** Cherry Enriquez
**Accounts Assistants** Soumyah Rajesh,
Sunil Suvarna
**Front Office Administrator**
Janette Tamayo
**Personnel Relations Officer** Rafi Jamal
**Office Assistant** Shafeer Ahamed

### IT & Digital Solutions
**Digital Solutions Manager**
Derrick Pereira
**Senior IT Administrator** R. Ajay
**Web Developer** Anas Abdul Latheef

# Contact Us

### ▶ Register Online
Check out our new website for event listings, competitions and Dubai info, and submit your own restaurant reviews.
Log onto **www.explorerpublishing.com/dubai**

### ▶ Newsletter
Register online to receive Explorer's monthly newsletter and be first in line for our special offers and competitions.
Log onto **www.explorerpublishing.com**

### ▶ General Enquiries
We'd love to hear your thoughts and answer any questions you have about this book or any other Explorer product.
Contact us at **info@explorerpublishing.com**

### ▶ Careers
If you fancy yourself as an Explorer, send your CV (stating the position you're interested in) to **jobs@explorerpublishing.com**

### ▶ Designlab and Contract Publishing
For enquiries about Explorer's Contract Publishing arm and design services contact **designlab@explorerpublishing.com**

### ▶ Maps
For cartography enquiries, including orders and comments, contact **maps@explorerpublishing.com**

### ▶ Media and Corporate Sales
For bulk sales and customisation options, for this book or any Explorer product, contact **sales@explorerpublishing.com**